# BECOMING A COUPLE OF DESTINY

# BECOMING A COUPLE OF DESTINY

## LIVING, LOVING, AND CREATING A LIFE THAT MATTERS

JOSEPH W. WALKER III
STEPHAINE HALE WALKER

Abingdon Press
*Nashville*

BECOMING A COUPLE OF DESTINY
LIVING, LOVING, AND CREATING A LIFE THAT MATTERS



*This book is printed on acid-free paper.*

**Library of Congress Cataloging-in-Publication Data**

Walker, Joseph Warren, 1967-
Becoming a couple of destiny : living, loving, and creating a life that matters / Joseph W. Walker III and Stephaine Hale Walker.
p. cm.
ISBN 978-1-4267-1198-5 (book -- hardback / with printed dust jacket : alk. paper)
1. Marriage—Religious aspects—Christianity. I. Walker, Stephaine Hale. II. Title.
BV835.W345 2011
248.8′44—dc23

2011034455

All scripture quotations unless noted otherwise are taken from the King James Version of the Bible.

11 12 13 14 15 16 17 18 19 20—10 9 8 7 6 5 4 3 2 1

MANUFACTURED IN THE UNITED STATES OF AMERICA

# Contents

# Acknowledgments

We are so grateful to so many wonderful persons who have been instrumental in our formation as individuals and as a couple.

To our amazing parents: Joseph and Rosa Walker of Shreveport, Louisiana, your persistence in parenting produced a son who would love and serve God and adore his wife; and to Jerry and Geraldine Hale of Los Angeles, California, your unending support and love produced an extraordinary woman whose gifts continue to touch lives around the world. We consider ourselves blessed to say that both sets of our parents have been married well over forty years. Your commitment to marriage remains our inspiration, and we are grateful for all the lessons you taught us.

We are thankful for our entire family. We are encouraged by your support and prayers as we attempt to touch the lives of God's people. We are forever grateful to all of our mentors too numerous to mention. You know who you are, and we hope that we are making you proud. Dr. John Borders, this book is possible because of your spiritual insight. You are truly a man sent from God, and we are eternally grateful that you introduced us.

To Dr. Harry Blake of the Mount Canaan Baptist Church of Shreveport, Louisiana: we will always be honored to call you Pastor.

To Bishop Paul S. Morton, our International Presiding Bishop: thank you and Pastor Debra for being stellar examples of integrity. You inspire us.

To the Mount Zion Baptist Church of Nashville, Tennessee: you guys are so amazing. Our love for you is indescribable. You pray for us and bless us in so many ways. We feel so honored to be connected to you, and we thank God that you are who you are. You are a gift from God to our lives, and we will always seek God's best for your lives.

All of our friends around the world, we are thankful for you. We hope that this book blesses you and your family in a special way. It is our desire to be used of God to help others in this journey called relationship. We are praying for you and truly believe that God's best will manifest in your life as you trust Him.

# FOREWORD

**By Bishop Paul S. Morton, Sr.**

THIS BOOK IS A REAL BLESSING. As a pastor for over thirty-five years and a married man for over thirty years, I recognize how necessary this subject matter is. So many successful people struggle with balancing the basic principles of life. We find that, all too often, people sacrifice their marriage on the altars of their careers or ministry. My wife, Debra, and I have lived with the demands of ministry and family for many years, and we understand the challenges that it can present. We have been successful in our marriage and our ministries because we have faced each challenge head-on and purposely developed spiritual responses and strategies.

When two people come together, they must recognize the importance of their witness in the kingdom of God. We all have been saddened by the numerous failed marriages among Christians and those who lead. This book is a must read because it addresses very practical issues and gives powerful solutions. One of my favorite scriptures is Isaiah 1:17: "Learn to do well." If our marriages are going to survive, we must invest in them through resources that empower us.

Many people live under the illusion that things are going to be easy once they enter into a covenant relationship with each other. What I appreciate about this book is that Bishop Walker and Dr. Stephaine have chosen to be transparent. It's rare when leaders in the church are transparent in sharing their struggles and painful moments and giving us insight into how they overcame them. As a Christian leader I have found in my life that transparency not only heals me but also helps others navigate through their personal situations. When I had my breakdown, I knew I had to be transparent so that people would understand the need to put life in proper order. God broke me to impress upon me the need for the spirit to be over the mind. When I suddenly lost my first granddaughter; then experienced hurricane Katrina, which destroyed our church and our home; then had to deal with a fire that destroyed another one of our churches; and had to face a bout with colon cancer, I used those moments not as lamentable moments of self-pity but as teaching moments to encourage the Body of Christ on how to make it through life's storms. We were one church in three locations, but we are now one church in two states. We never gave up or threw in the towel because we knew God had a greater plan for our lives. It's during those times that my marriage and ministry were strengthened. Debra now pastors in New Orleans, and I pastor in Atlanta—and we make it work. We are committed to doing God's will and loving each other in a way that brings Him glory in the kingdom of God.

I am so proud of my spiritual son, Bishop Joseph Walker. I've watched him go through numerous experiences. I've seen him go through his ministry being displaced by people who didn't appreciate where God was leading him, experience the loss of his first wife, Diane, deal with a house fire and then a historic flood in Nashville, and yet demonstrate tremendous character through it all. After his first wife passed, he maintained incredible integrity and waited on God to send him a wife. When Stephaine came into his life, I knew God had restored him. To see their witness is a true inspiration.

Whatever challenges you face in your marriage, this book will be of great benefit to you. Or, if you are considering marriage and want to learn strategies that successful people employ, this book is for you as well.

So many marriages are under attack, and we need spiritual people to show us how to make it. I believe God is raising up another generation of leaders with integrity and insight to speak to a culture that has become cynical about marriage. When you have a successful physician and pastor, like Dr. Stephaine and Bishop Walker, share their journey and provide biblical principles, it is necessary that you take advantage of it. Though the kingdom is under so much attack, I am encouraged that there are voices God is raising up to speak to righteousness in covenant. There are those who enjoy marriage and who are making it work every day.

Debra and I love each other more today than we did yesterday. We've had our challenges, but we chose to fight for our marriage and develop a system that would work for us. God has granted us grace over these years because we have been as intentional about investing in our marriage as we have in our ministry. As you pursue your dreams and strive to be successful in your respective fields, remember that your first ministry is at home. You can't get an "A" at work and an "F" at home.

Thank God for Bishop Joseph Walker and Lady Stephaine. This book is for anyone who lives at a fast pace and is committed to making their marriage work. When you read this book, it will become increasingly clear that you are not alone in your struggles. You will be enlightened, challenged, and empowered. This is a book that should be required reading for any couple before getting married and for anyone who is already married. I thank God for how it has blessed me, and I know it will be a blessing to you.

—Bishop Paul S. Morton, Sr.
Changing a Generation
Full Gospel Baptist Church, Senior Pastor
Presiding Bishop, Full Gospel Baptist Church
Fellowship International

Chapter 1

# Our Story: Beginning in God's Garden of Destiny

## BETTER TOGETHER

THIS BOOK IS ABOUT becoming a couple of destiny and understanding how to successfully negotiate your life as a couple. God brought you together for a purpose. That purpose is greater than your own individual purpose, and God wants to put you both on a path that will lead to fulfillment, peace, and abundant joy—in short, your destiny. While you may be great as separate individuals—leading full, meaningful lives—you have committed to live together as a couple. You have promised to love, cherish, and keep each other; and, most likely, you made these promises in front of your family and friends. But no matter where or when you became a couple, you also made these promises before our ever-present God. The message of this book is that you can be better together than you ever were separately and that by walking together in God's will for your life, you will find your destiny and establish your home in peace.

Although people often approach relationships with selfish motives, we soon discover that God's will for our lives is far greater than we imagined. Paul says in 2 Corinthians 4:1, "Therefore, seeing we have this ministry, as we have received mercy, we faint not." Paul's word to this Corinthian church charges them to see beyond themselves. Once you truly see and understand God's will, you can see beyond yourself and recognize that God strategically connects you to people who will help you grow into the person God wants you to be.

In this book Stephaine and I share our story. Sometimes you'll see that we have different perspectives on the same story. But we begin each chapter together, and we conclude each chapter together with some talking points for you. We hope that you and your spouse read this book, do the exercises, and answer the questions at the end of the chapters, so that you can discover the exquisite gift you can be to each other. While we are attempting to "walk the walk" and not just talk, we also realize that we are not perfect people nor do we make the perfect couple. In fact, we still consider ourselves newlyweds in some respects, but we believe that even through some of our mistakes, you will see two people striving to be a couple of destiny. We also hope that you will allow us to walk beside you as you walk in God's purpose toward the destiny He has for you.

Before we met, Stephaine and I were individually successful in our own lives, but God brought us together to do, like you, something awesome for His glory. Paul says we faint not. We never get tired or worn out by the process, because God grants us mercy when we fail and when we succeed. Relationships and marriages of destiny are truly a ministry of God's unending mercy, because two imperfect people come together to walk in the way that leads to life. And this can only happen when individuals and couples come to a place of total reliance upon God. This means that we make a commitment to put God first in our marriage. Because, when we do, God is in a better position to give us the good gifts He intends for us.

Considering the events in our pasts, Stephaine and I had to rely totally upon God. I had lost a wife and, admittedly, I had become cynical about the possibility of loving again. Stephaine had become cynical about whether true love even existed. Though our connection was truly a divine orchestration, our spirits were tired. But it's often in those moments of hopelessness and fatigue that we can witness the power of God the most. Total reliance upon God eradicated all our fears and doubts, and allowed us to grow together through our courtship and in our marriage. Solomon says in Proverbs 3:5 that we should "trust in the LORD with all thine heart; and lean not unto thine own understanding."

## RELIABLE REFERENCES

THERE ARE TWO FOUNDATIONAL PRINCIPLES that enable us to trust. The first is reliable reference. We would never hire a person without getting references from a reliable source, and we usually take that source's advice and place our trust in the people we hire based on what others have said. When you read the Bible, you see hundreds of reliable references that speak to the benefit of trusting God. The writer in Hebrews calls them "so great a cloud of witnesses" (12:1). These are those whose testimonies and stories encourage us to trust God beyond what has been and believe God for what is to come in our *Now* and in our *Not Yet*.

### PERSONAL EXPERIENCES

THE SECOND THING THAT ENFORCES OUR TRUST is personal experience. When we look back over our own lives, we can begin to see a pattern. God allows us to go through a series of experiences in order that we may come to trust Him. Without those challenging experiences, we would never know the power of reliance. Every bad relationship in your past has been instrumental in helping you trust God now. Rather than become bitter, you should thank God that it has made you better and that you have profited from your experience. Both reliable references and personal experience were important to how our own relationship as a couple unfolded. We trust God with our *Now*, and we trust God with our *Not Yet*.

## JOSEPH'S STORY

THE BEGINNING OF OUR RELATIONSHIP was really something that began before Stephaine and I even met. That's how God works. I am convinced that before the foundations of the world, God was at work bringing us together at the right time and in the right place in order to impact the world in a positive way. As Adam had been prepared for Eve and she for him, God prepares us for each other, and God has prepared you for each other. Look over the pattern of your life and see how it has brought you to your mate.

If we had connected *before* our appointed time, things would not have happened as they did. Stephaine was a member of Mount Zion Church when she was an undergraduate student. While she was at Vanderbilt she attended services regularly, but we never met. Our church was growing so fast that students would come get the Word and then leave right after church. By the time I was shaking hands after the service, many of them were already back on campus. And during that time I was married and clearly in another place in my life. If Stephaine and I had met, even casually, it would have probably been weird, to say the least, for us to connect years later.

## *Right Time, Right Season for Every Good Thing*

The blessing is that God's hand was in it the whole time. Even though I knew many of her friends, I never met her until the day we were introduced by her pastor in Boston years later. Truly there is a time and a season for everything, and we have to be willing to wait for God to navigate circumstances rather than get in His way.

If you find yourself discouraged, wondering if you are ever going to connect with the right person, be of good cheer. God is at work in your life. And as my mother-in-law so eloquently says, "What you are looking for is looking for you." Destiny really exists for those who are willing to trust God's creative power.

I believe that the events of my life were preordained by God to bring me to a place where I would be open to meeting someone of Stephaine's caliber and moving toward destiny with her. I had just come through years of emotional unrest. When you've experienced the loss of a spouse, your spirit is closed and you can't imagine life beyond the acute crisis you are facing. For me it took three long years to even reconnect with myself. The expectations of the ministry were so overwhelming that I knew I needed to take a step back and breathe.

### *God Is Always Working and Creating Destiny*

When I think of the creative work of God in Genesis, I understand that before the beginning there was God. The beginning is literally the culmination of God's activity in the creative act. The moment I met Stephaine, I recognized God's hand. God had been working on me—shifting me, molding me, and preparing me for what lay ahead.

In 2007, I remember sitting in a chair in my great room contemplating whether I would remain single or pursue another relationship. I must admit that I thought long and hard about this decision; however, deep inside I knew I was wired for relationship. There were numerous introductions and encounters that had led me to this place. But it was when I stopped looking that God delivered on the promise that "it is not good that the man should be alone" (Genesis 2:18). I was speaking at a pastor's conference in Orlando, Florida, when Dr. John Borders, a pastor of a great church in Boston, approached me between sessions. I never will forget his words. He was certain that the Lord had laid it upon his heart to introduce me to someone. I had heard that statement so many times before, but this was different. His sincerity was genuine and unique. I felt myself yield, and when I did, I was certain that my life had changed forever.

### *Destiny Chooses You to Be a Couple*

The thing I've learned about destiny is that you don't choose it. It chooses you. When you've been prepared, then God moves. This is what God did in the garden in the beginning. Everything was in proper order; I had been sufficiently molded by His hands, and then God moved in my life in the area of relationship. When Dr. Borders told me about Stephaine, I was impressed. Although my flesh stepped in briefly to Google her to see what she looked like. Though we both laugh at that even today, I realize that her outward beauty is matched by her inner beauty and spirit beyond anything I could have ever imagined.

I remember the first time we talked. We spoke for hours. I had not known that she had attended my church years ago when she was an undergraduate. Though we had not really met, it was comforting knowing that I had contributed to her spiritual life during a pivotal season for her. How amazing was this? God had positioned Stephaine under my ministry and allowed my heart for God to be known to her without really ever meeting me.

### *Being Equally Yoked*

During our lengthy conversations early in our relationship, it was obvious that we were equally yoked. Being single for so long made me sensitive to the desperation and unwise decisions of people who desire a relationship—any relationship. God clearly had prepared me for this moment. I was so ready and so impressed with her spiritual sensitivity and desire to be in the will of God for her life that it is difficult for me to imagine how this journey toward destiny could even begin without a relationship with Jesus Christ. Without His teaching, direction, and guidance, it is frustrating at best to try to connect with the person God has for you.

### *Transparent Communication*

As we got to know each other, I was impressed with the depth of my conversations with Stephaine. They revealed a lot, but they also created a sense of transparency and honesty. When two people connect, communication is vital to the well-being of the relationship. I counsel so many couples and single folks who struggle with communication. The blessing in getting to know Stephaine was that our communication was organic; it was natural. It flowed because we shared similar passions, hopes, and desires. One moment we were discussing politics and the next education. It was refreshing to meet someone who was well versed in a variety of fields. The depth of communication was also a clear indication to me that our relationship was evolving beyond friendship.

### *Iron Sharpens Iron*

The way we communicate says a lot about our character and our potential. I came to grips with the fact some time ago that my initial attraction to Stephaine was intellectual because of her easy communication style. When you are progressive—that is, moving in God's purpose toward your destiny—and your mind is actively engaged, you are attracted to people who challenge you and stretch you beyond your comfort zone. Relationships should add value to you. Iron sharpens iron. You need people in your life who can motivate you and bring out your best rather than allow you to stagnate. We challenge each other and inspire each other. When it's destiny, you know that God has placed something in that person and something in you for each other. My worldview was changing and my level of sensitivity was increasing all because of the wonderful conversations Stephaine and I had.

### *When I Knew She Was the One*

People ask me all the time, "When did you know?" When was it apparent that I would be with this woman? I must admit that even prior to meeting her, I fell in love just by talking on the phone. I knew she was the one when I could be open about my pain and she assured me that she would cover me in it. She gave me the liberty to discuss anything that was on my mind. Talking to her became cathartic. No matter what was going on in my hectic day, once I got on the phone with her, everything was at peace. It was my refuge.

If your relationship does not give you peace, I am convinced that it is not of God. He is not the author of confusion; He is the author of peace. This doesn't suggest that Stephaine and I didn't have disagreements; however, we were able to work through them because of our ability to communicate on so many levels. No matter what was said, I came to know her heart and she mine because we invested in our communication. I knew she was the one, because I knew her. How much do you invest in your communication? Does it need to have higher priority in your relationship?

### *The Challenge of Communication*

One of the things I have discovered in ministering to couples is that communication is a significant challenge, partly because they give it such low priority and partly because they don't have that skill set. Because many people struggle with communication, they rely instead on unhealthy assumptions, which can hinder the relationship from developing in a healthy way. Unhealthy assumptions can also create a great deal of suspicion and hesitancy within the relationship based on bad past experiences. One way to avoid assumptions is just by being open about asking and answering questions. Stephaine and I came to know each other because we were intentional about asking appropriate questions and answering questions that were asked, because unasked and unanswered questions can linger over a relationship and prevent it from becoming all that God desires.

After Stephaine and I talked on the phone for an entire month, I knew it was time for us to meet. I've heard people say that they have fallen in love with a person prior to meeting them face to face, but I had my reservations. I knew I had feelings, but I was a little unprepared to find out how deep they really were. It's in moments like these that God will literally blow your mind. He certainly blew mine.

### *Being Open to God's Ideas about Your Destiny*

I will never forget that flight to Boston. I had a great deal of anxiety, because I knew that my life was about to change forever. I was about to meet this woman who had wowed me and given me a reason to love again. I was nervous the entire flight. The path to destiny is not without anxiety. I know that God does not give us the spirit of fear but of power, love, and a sound mind; however, when you are about to experience a significant shift in your life, it can bring up unmanageable emotions in the best of us. I often wonder what Abram felt in Genesis 12 when God told him to make a significant shift in his life. To leave the confines of what you've decided is normal and open yourself up to God's great unknown can be unnerving to say the least.

I remember hearing God say to me in that moment on the plane, "Do you trust me?" How did I know God's voice? I knew it because when you've been through what I've been through, you become accustomed to the voice that has guided you through tumultuous times. I had to truly trust that God knew what was best for me and that this flight, this encounter, was all preordained by Him. When I accepted and embraced this fully, I found peace.

When you come to recognize that you are in the will of God and that where you are is a part of a larger plan for your life, you will find refuge in that moment. God told Jeremiah that He was up to something in his life before his mother conceived him in her womb. It was clear to me that everything that had happened in my life had led me to this place. I took great comfort in God's promise made in Romans 8:28, "And we know that all things work together for good to them that love God, to them who are the called according to his purpose." Even so, that relatively short, two-hour flight seemed like a trip across the ocean. But it was necessary in order for me to approach meeting Stephaine in peace and not in panic.

When I arrived in Boston, I was not alone. Two of my assistants had traveled with me. And although they said they wanted to stay in the city, I really think they had perceived my nervousness and wanted to go with me for support. Whatever the case, I was glad they came. It's great to have people in your life who genuinely love you and want the best for you. I felt so blessed. But although they were with me, I knew that I would have to approach the moment of truth alone. Stephaine was at work when I arrived, and our meeting wouldn't take place for another hour at the hotel. When I received a call that she was downstairs, my palms were sweaty and my heart raced with anticipation. As it happened, my room was on one of the top floors, so even the ride down in the elevator seemed endless.

Again I was immersed in intense contemplation. My entire life ran across my mind in the long three minutes it took to get to the lobby. When I arrived, I looked around—and then I saw her. Her back was to me, and she was on the phone. I later discovered that she was experiencing the same anxiety. She was on the phone with her mother, who was coaching and comforting her. I immediately approached her, and when she turned around and we made eye contact, I knew instantly that this was it. I knew that my destiny had come full circle. I knew in that split second that this woman was put on the planet for me and I for her. I knew that our lives from that moment would be permanently intertwined. There was no escaping this. This was God's work. Our destiny was here and now.

### *Giving Us Our Heart's Desire*

I was blessed to find a woman to whom I was attracted at every level. I remember making a list and holding fast to God's promise in Psalm 37 that He will give us the desires of our heart. But so many folks miss this fundamental principle. God gives you the grace to trust Him when you ask Him specifically for what you want. People can try to make you feel guilty for asking, but you know you better than anyone else. You know the kind of person that you will be compatible with. It's okay to be specific with God and offer supplications in this area. In fact, it can be frustrating to settle for anything less than God's best for you. But each person is unique and has to come to this place for themselves. A lot of people will call you unrealistic, and you might be. Nevertheless, you must pray about what you desire in your life and submit that to God.

### *A Suitable Helpmeet for Your "Not Yet"*

The beauty of what God did in the Garden of Eden is that He made Adam a mate *suitable for him*. Eve could not have been anyone's wife but Adam's, because God knew what Adam needed. So often when folks make a list about what they are looking for and submit it to God, they write down what they want rather than what they need. But God will respond to what we really need. There is a reason for this. God doesn't connect us to people in serious relationship for our "right now"; God creates a relationship for our "not yet." He knows how our lives are going to evolve, and He strategically connects us to people who can handle where we are going. There are some great people who will love you and be kind to you. What you will sadly discover, however, is that when your life changes, they won't be able to make the adjustments necessary to support you on the trajectory your life will take.

When God brought Stephaine and me together, He did so because He knew that she would be a tremendous support to me in regard to where He was taking me. He knew that I would be a great support to her as well. He will take us together where we cannot go alone without each other. There is great comfort in knowing that God sees all and knows all. He is in control. Once we learn that lesson, our lives run smoother.

## *The Most Powerful Gift*

Stephaine and I enjoyed each other's company that day we met in person. Walking through the Copley Center in Boston was an event. One of the coolest things we discovered about each other was how we could just be ourselves. There is an assumption we all make that if we try to impress people, it will help our chances. What I learned is that *being you* is the most powerful gift you can give someone. For example, when Stephaine asked me where I wanted to eat lunch, I could have tried to impress her and suggest an ultra-expensive five-star restaurant, but my response was simply: Cheesecake Factory. I thought in that moment that I had said the most wonderful thing because her expression was sheer relief. She told me how refreshing it was to have someone in her life who enjoyed the same things she did.

Men, you don't have to go broke trying to impress someone. Do the best you can and be honest about what you enjoy. You might be pleasantly surprised how much you and your mate have in common. Although five-stars have their place, it's incredibly important to the relationship that you never get away from who you are, void of the "stuff" attached to you. That's who your mate needs to know. So often we make the mistake of only connecting with people through the things that are attached to us. The problem becomes that they never get to know who we really are. They may know all about the stuff in our lives. Our home, car, income, and business connections begin to define their perception of who we really are. There is nothing wrong with nice things, but you cannot allow them to define who you are. At the end of the day, the person who God has brought into your life for destiny will be with you even if you lose everything. That's where real love exists.

### *In-To-Me-To-See*

While we were getting to know each other, Stephaine refused to Google me. She didn't want any preconceived notions in her head about who I was and what I had. She wanted to know me, Joseph. The fact that she wasn't concerned with who Bishop Joseph Warren Walker III was but rather wanted to know Joseph, the man, immediately confirmed to me her sincere motivation to get to know me.

In my book *Love and Intimacy,* I discussed how true intimacy is *In-To-Me-To-See.* When Adam looked at Eve, he said she was "bone of my bones, and flesh of my flesh" (Genesis 2:23). He worked his way from the inside out. Bone is internal and flesh is external. *In-To-Me-To-See* means that when we love someone, we are able see beyond the exterior and truly embrace the essence of who a person really is. I am convinced that many people meet folks and show up with their "representative." What I mean by this is that it's a big masquerade. You never know who you are getting when you meet some people. When people are genuinely interested in you, they will invest time in getting to know you from the inside out rather than from the outside in. This is what separates serious relationships from those that are shallow. How impressed are you with external appearances? Are they more important to you than what is on the inside of a person? As we get older, the externals change, but the internal qualities of a person mature, mellow, and can grow richer and more valuable.

## *Season of Discovery*

As Stephaine and I continued to nurture our relationship, we experienced an amazing season of discovery, which continues even today. Each day we learn more and more about each other. Relationships are constantly evolving because we constantly change. That's why it's important to have someone in your life who can grow with you. As our life as a couple grows, it becomes more apparent that we are in each other's lives to keep growing together.

Some people come into our lives for a reason and others for a season. When the space shuttle launches into outer space, a marvelous thing happens. There are two rocket boosters attached to the side of the shuttle. Once it reaches a certain altitude, the rocket boosters fall off. To the unlearned eye, it appears that there is a malfunction; however, this is a perfectly normal part of the flight process. Those rocket boosters are designed to fall off at a certain altitude: they were never designed to fly in orbit. They serve their purpose in helping the shuttle get to a certain level; then they fall off.

This is how some relationships will be in your life. Some people are in your life to help you get to a certain level—nothing wrong with them and nothing wrong with you. But in a certain season, they will fall off, because they aren't meant to go into your orbit. Where God is about to take you, you will require somebody who has been ordained to navigate at that altitude. I knew without a doubt that Stephaine and I were in each other's lives for good.

### *Connecting with God as a Couple*

Stephaine and I realized that our connection was divine. We treated it as such and made sure that we prayed every day. We continue this today. There is no way God is going to connect you to someone of destiny and the devil not attack it. This is why it's important to put a spiritual covering around your relationship and marriage. We pray fervently that God will protect us and allow us to walk in wisdom, so that we don't give the enemy a place in our lives.

Your relationship must be protected and nurtured spiritually. If it is going to grow and become what God intended, you cannot take this area for granted. Christ must be the center of your relationship if it is to have sustainability. Because we prayed daily from the beginning, Christ became our point of reference whenever there were disagreements in our relationship. We constantly sought His will in regard to what He needed us to be for each other. I remember praying, "Lord, make me the man that she needs in her life." I know she prayed a similar prayer. There is no harm in praying that God will continue to mold you and shape you into the person you need to be for your mate. I prayed this prayer because I knew we were both changing. Marriage is a ministry, and my understanding of ministry is simple—meeting needs. If I was going to meet Stephaine's needs, I had to be the man who could do so without hesitation. I needed God to connect me to her spirit and her needs. He did that, and we both enjoy a connection far beyond anything we've ever experienced in our lives.

We also both prayed for each other. We spent quality time seeking God about the next chapter of our lives. Stephaine had come through a series of painful long-term relationships, and I had suffered the loss of a spouse. Before meeting Stephaine, I remember sitting in my living room crying out to God, asking Him about the next chapter of my life. I had come to a point of resignation, and it was then that I heard God tell me that was the place He desired me to be—to totally remove my hand from the process and know that He had heard me.

Meeting Stephaine was the result of praying for her. Though I did not know her name, I knew that the woman who would spend the rest of my life with me was in my spirit. When I prayed, I believe that something literally happened. When you pray and it seems like nothing is happening, don't believe it. God is always moving. The devil wants you to believe that your prayers have fallen on deaf ears. Matthew 7:7 says, "Ask, and it shall be given you; seek, and ye shall find; knock, and it shall be opened unto you." I refused to let frustration set in. I believed God for it and stood on His promise. I know firsthand that when God makes you a promise, He will make good on it.

When you pray and it seems like nothing is happening, don't believe it. God is always moving.

It's amazing how many couples connect but don't spend time praying, and then they wonder why they can't ward off the attacks of the enemy. Stephaine and I are in agreement spiritually, and whenever there is an attack, she knows that we are going to address it spiritually. Paul says in 2 Corinthians 10:4, "The weapons of our warfare are not carnal, but mighty through God to the pulling down of strong holds." When you pray, you stay connected to God's will for your life and place a spiritual fence around your relationship as a couple.

It doesn't matter how spiritual you are or how much you feel connected to each other, attacks will come. We refuse to allow the enemy to break us; rather we get stronger and stronger through each attack. What each attack does is give us opportunity to learn more about each other. It gives us an opportunity to focus and learn more about ourselves. It keeps us on our knees, looking forward.

Becoming a couple of destiny means that your focus is on the destination—your destiny. When you run a race, how you start is important, and you must start with your eye on the finish line—your goal. How you start can be a determining factor in how you finish. When you are in the embryonic stages of your relationship, it is important to nurture it and protect it, because you have the end in mind—a God-given gift. Is your eye on the finish line, and are you and your mate running toward it rather than running off-track, chasing something that will take you far afield?

## *God Invests in Us*

As we progress in our relationship and marriage, Stephaine and I understand what is necessary to protect our relationship. God has made a significant investment in us. It's only when you recognize God's investment in the two of you coming together that you will value it enough to protect it. Just as God invested in a garden and put Adam and Eve in it, God makes an investment in your life. This is why God preserved you until this moment of destiny. God has great plans for your life. Jeremiah 29:11 says, "I know the thoughts that I think toward you... thoughts of peace, and not of evil, to give you an expected end." When you know you have prayed and God has answered, start out on the right foot. Have strong communication and move beyond the surface to the significant. Get to know each other genuinely and embrace transparency. Ask the right questions and be willing to answer the tough questions.

Take a few minutes and think about your relationship with your spouse. How well do you really know each other? How much time do you spend together? What things do you need or want in your relationship that you are getting and that you are not getting? These questions are meant to be not an indictment of you or your spouse but an honest assessment of your marriage. Might you benefit from a marriage enrichment program or even counseling?

****

## Stephaine's Story

In April 2008, I was in a hotel room in Philadelphia, Pennsylvania, preparing to take my Neonatology board exam the following day with a couple hundred other young physicians. I remember feeling extremely spent—spiritually taxed and mentally and emotionally exhausted. I had been crying for the past few minutes when I was startled by a knock at the door. I quickly remembered that I had ordered room service not long ago. After gaining my composure and wiping the tears from my eyes, I answered the door. An older woman—petite, in her late fifties—appeared. I tried to hide my emotions with a big smile as she rolled the tray with my dinner on it into the room.

Around that same time my laptop sitting on the desk had gone into sleep mode, allowing rotating pictures of friends and family to populate the screen. She looked over and saw a picture of a gentleman flash on the screen. "Your husband?" she asked. "No," I tried to say in the most nonchalant way I could muster.

"What's next for me? What am I doing wrong? Why do I keep running into Mr. Wrong, Mr. Unavailable, Mr. Immature?"

Little did she know that I was in the process of separating myself from one of the most unfruitful relationships I had ever been in. Not only was I so very much NOT married, I wasn't even dating anyone anymore. I could lie right now and say I felt wonderful about it—but I didn't. Do you want to know why I was crying? I had been crying earlier because I had been on my knees praying and asking God, "What's next for me? What am I doing wrong? Why do I keep running into Mr. Wrong, Mr. Unavailable, Mr. Immature?" What did I need to do to be where God wanted me to be so that He could deliver to me my soul mate? My king? My helpmeet? What did I need to work on to be a better me in preparation for Mr. Wonderful? Because at this point Mr. Picture was a big zero, and I was tired of encountering guys who were into playing games and wasting my time.

Of course, I didn't tell the woman who brought the food any of this. I just kept smiling and nodding as she made small talk about the beautiful weather outside. As the woman left the room and I was closing the door behind her, she stopped suddenly (somewhat startling me), turned around and pointed to the computer, looked me directly in the eyes, and said, "Don't worry about him. You can't let him get you down. God has someone amazing in store for you; you just wait." And with that, she turned and walked away. All I could do was stand there, stunned and speechless.

As I closed the door, I could hear God tell me just as plain as if you and I were talking, "You have not, because you ask not!" Of course, I was a bit confused because I knew beyond a shadow of a doubt that I HAD asked God for someone special to spend the rest of my life with. He said to me, yes, you have asked, but at the same time you have always been very vague, saying, "Any way you bless me, I'll be fine." I always felt that by doing so I was honoring God's sovereignty and allowing Him to bring into my life whomever He saw fit for me. But God revealed to me that that wasn't the truth at all. Instead, He helped me see that the REAL reason I was so vague was because I was afraid to ask Him for what I really wanted—perhaps out of fear that that person didn't exist or, even worse, out of fear that He couldn't create a person who fit all of my desires. He said, "Dare to trust me like you say you do—write it down, make it plain, and know that I can bring forth the desires of your heart. Don't you dare limit what I can do based on your own limited human knowledge.

Know that I am GOD and I can do ALL things, if you believe. It's up to you." Needless to say, I was blown away!

What are you asking God for? Are you being specific? Will you dare to trust Him more? Are you ready for God to blow your mind?

### *Patience and Discipline to Wait on God*

That evening, I sat on the bed in the hotel room, opened my journal, and began to write. No one can ever say I didn't act on what God spoke to me. I thought about all of the desires of my heart. I asked myself, "In an ideal world, what would I want in a mate?" and with that, I put those things on paper. Well, four pieces of paper later, I finally came up for air. I never understood that I had all of that inside of me. I knew I was writing not because God didn't already know what I hoped for in a mate but instead as a test of my faith. Did I have faith to believe that God would deliver on HIS word? Boy, did I ever! That wasn't the question. The real question would be, would I have the patience and discipline to wait on God?

Well, let's just say, when you finally do act on what God tells you to do, He then can move on that promise. One thing I've come to realize is that we often feel that we are waiting on God, but the reality is that God is often waiting on us to do what He has asked us to do. So, fast-forward four weeks: I'm at work when my phone rings, and it's my pastor, John Borders III. Yes, I was a little bit surprised but thought, he's just checking on me. He mentioned a friend of his was coming to town, and he wanted me to join them for lunch. I didn't think anything of it, as Rev. Borders knew I was living in Boston by myself and was involved in medicine and health policy. He was always introducing me to people after church in order to get me better connected in the city. I thought he was just trying to help me network in that regard, so I said, "Yes, of course."

A few days later Rev. Borders called me back and asked if there was a website people could go to in order to find out more information about me—again, I was thinking "professional website" with my bio for networking purposes—so I gave him a few. Then he asked, "Do any of these have pictures of you?" At that moment I got a little uneasy, thinking, "Hey, should he be asking me that?" However, being the discerning man of God he is, he says, "No, no—it's not for me!" It was then that it dawned on me for the first time what he was up to. "Wait a minute!" I said, "Are you trying to set me up with someone?" Well, yes, he was. And no, I was not interested. I had never gone on a blind date nor allowed any of my friends or family to set me up. So, no, thank you, I was fine.

Immediately Rev. Borders began telling me how great this young man was—a man of God, a person of utmost integrity, and so on. Then he said, "His name is Joe Walker, and he's a preacher out of Nashville." The name sounded familiar. It took me a second to place it, but then I was shocked! I immediately told my pastor that I had gone to Joseph's church when I was an undergrad at Vanderbilt University. As God would have it, I never actually met him despite regularly attending his church for three years. My friends and I would go to church, get the

Word, then leave right after the benediction and return to school to study. Those were honestly some of the most formative years of my spiritual growth and development.

When I realized who my pastor was referring to, I told him no way. I didn't think it was appropriate to date my old pastor. Rev. Borders went on to tell me how wonderful Joseph was, how he had gotten to know him over time, and how he felt that we had a lot in common. He insisted that I just HAD to meet this man, saying, "Now, THIS is the kind of man you give the time of day to." He had met a previous acquaintance of mine and never really approved—and did not hesitate telling me so.

By the end of the phone call, he made me promise that I would at least talk to Joseph over the phone.

By the end of the phone call, he made me promise that I would at least talk to Joseph over the phone. "Fine," I said. I was thinking OK, maybe he would call me in a week or so, but no, uh-uh, five minutes later my phone rang. It was Joseph! It was a little awkward at first, but Joseph very quickly made me feel comfortable. He started to comment on some of the things Rev. Borders had told him about me, but then he started mentioning things that you could only find in my bio or my CV. Partially offended and taken aback, I asked, "Did you Google me?" His response: "Of course I did! There are a lot of crazies out here!" I couldn't help laughing, and from that moment on, he had me. We spoke to each other every day, multiple times a day, for hours at a time.

### *"Getting" Each Other*

Although Joseph Googled me and I had thought to do the same, I never did. I came to the conclusion, and told Joseph, that I didn't want to get to know the Joseph that the world knew. I understood that he was likely quite accomplished, and I didn't want to take anything away from that: I simply wanted to get to know the Joseph that exists "behind closed doors," so to speak. I was only interested in those things he was willing to share with me. I found myself able to talk to Joseph about everything, and he "got me"—he understood me and how I thought, the way my mind works, my life philosophies, what makes me tick, as well as what ticks me off. But just as important, I found myself intrigued by his life's story and our discussions about everything. We found that we were so much alike. I often described him to my friends as a male version of myself. I knew I was in love less than two weeks after meeting over the phone. I knew he was "the one" well before we met in person.

As Joseph said, we actually didn't meet in person until he came up to Boston to preach at my home church, Morningstar Baptist, about a month after our first conversation. I tell you, it was well worth the wait. We talked about EVERYTHING. We adopted a motto, "Full Transparency," where anything and everything could be asked and discussed. I have to tell you that when I finally did see him for the first time, I could hardly breathe. I know it sounds corny, but I saw him coming toward me from across the room and literally had to turn my back to him to gain my composure. I have never in my life been nervous to meet anyone. When I turned back around, he was standing right in front of me. There was a quickening in my spirit then—I knew that I was staring at my future husband.

While courting, integrating our worlds was not difficult at all. Amazingly, everything had been so easy, yet another sign that God has His hand all over our relationship. When we look back at how hectic our schedules were—all of our respective commitments, the long distance, long work hours—anyone would expect it to be anything but easy. But that's how you know it's GOD—it's seemingly effortless. We never could have orchestrated this ourselves. For instance, with our careers: although different in many ways, they are quite similar in some respects. Joseph is called to save souls. He deals with healing from the spiritual perspective. I've been called to save lives and deal with healing from a physical perspective. Although different they're quite similar and oftentimes, even in the hospital, our worlds merge. Additionally, with our innate passions, such as making a difference in the community, mentoring young people, "lifting as we climb," seeking equality for vulnerable populations—whether on the level of economics, education, healthcare, or housing—we are on the same page. So much of what we do appears superficially different; yet when you look a little closer, our passions are perfectly aligned. We talked all the time about how God had clearly brought us together for something much bigger than ourselves. But that's how God usually works. He doesn't often bless for the sake of blessing. He blesses so that you may be a blessing to others, and that's exactly what we planned to do: continue to allow ourselves to be used for God's kingdom.

### *Plans and Surprises*

My birthday is September 17. That year it happened to be on a Wednesday. The day before, Joseph had thirty-three beautiful long-stem roses delivered to my home with a card that said, "33 roses for the 33 years God has blessed this world with you." Simply beautiful! The next day, my birthday, he was speaking at a church in Atlanta, so I flew down after work to have dinner with him, the pastor of the church, and the pastor's wife. We had dinner at a wonderful seafood restaurant. After dinner, we took a drive and Joseph had cake and other desserts waiting for us. Then, out of nowhere, he starts pulling out HUGE boxes for me to unwrap. I was stunned. I cried as I opened the gifts. He is so amazingly thoughtful. What more could I ask for? I was done! The best birthday I've ever had, right? Wrong, because unbeknownst to me, it wasn't over yet.

The next day, Thursday, we flew down to Shreveport to visit his mom, who was in the hospital but was doing better, so Friday we flew back to Atlanta because we had planned to drive back to Nashville. On the way, we stopped in Chattanooga, Tennessee. He took me to Lookout Mountain, where we walked around Rock City, which is gorgeous. There's even an area where you can see seven states from one spot. We also went to Ruby Falls, which is a beautiful underground waterfall.

Later that evening we continued on to Nashville, arriving in the city around 10:30 at night. We walked in the house, and out of nowhere, "SURPRISE!" What? A surprise birthday party? I couldn't take any more! More tears! I looked around, and there were new friends and old friends alike. He even managed to have family and friends from all over the country, some as far as the Virgin Islands, fly in for the festivities. I had no idea! As I walked around and greeted people (still in tears, mind you) I realized the music I was hearing was great, and would you believe, I looked up and saw a singer and a live band playing on the balcony. I walked into the kitchen—there was a chef cooking food for everyone! I was still spinning when someone came up behind me and whispered in my ear that they didn't want me to pass out but to turn around because behind me on the bookshelves surrounding the fireplace were "33 gifts for 33 years." I know. Unbelievable! I can't say it enough.

"SURPRISE!" What? A surprise birthday party? I couldn't take any more!

We had an amazing time celebrating and fellowshipping with friends and family. After all the guests left, I stayed up with my sister and close friends from out of town all night and opened presents. The next morning was Saturday, and to my surprise more of my friends flew in! Joseph had really outdone himself. He, my sister, my friends, and I went to breakfast at one of our favorite restaurants. We then took them on a tour of the city and hung out for the remainder of the day. Those who stayed went out to dinner with us that night at one of Nashville's best steakhouses. When we arrived, we had a private room where there were roses and candles everywhere. It was beautiful. We had a wonderful dinner.

We laughed and talked about the week's events. I noticed that Joseph was starting to "zone out" a little. However, I attributed that to the fact that we CLEARLY had had a very exciting week and he was winding down in preparation for Sunday, as he usually does around this time. Next thing I know, he steps out to use his phone, then comes back into the room and begins to give this soliloquy about how much he loves me and how much I mean to him. At this point, I could not even begin to imagine him planning anything else after the week we just had, so I just thought he was making sure that before my friends and family left they truly knew his heart and how much he loved me. Right? Wrong again.

Suddenly he turned to me and said, "I also spoke to your father today." I stopped short and sort of looked at him sideways and asked him, "Why did you speak to my father today?" His reply: "To ask for your hand in marriage." All I remember after that was hearing my sister and girlfriends screaming hysterically on the other side of the table. I could not see anything in the room except Joseph, my eyes were fixed solidly on him, and the rest was slow motion. I saw him stand up, walk around his seat, reach into his bag, and pull out a blue box. He then got down on one knee and asked me if I would marry him. Of course, crying by this point, I shouted, "ABSOLUTELY, ABSOLUTELY, ABSOLUTELY!" I threw my arms around his neck. My head was spinning! When I look back, I realize that Joseph was really proposing to me the entire week: the flowers, the dinner, the gifts in Atlanta, taking me to the highest points and standing by me in the lowest points, bringing together the fellowship of friends and family—all to propose! God is so good. When you dare to trust and believe—that's when God just takes the opportunity to show out!

****

## JOURNEY OF DISCOVERY

FROM THE VERY BEGINNING even until now, we set out to know as much about each other as we could, not as Bishop and Dr. but as Joseph and Stephaine. For us, it's a journey of discovery. When we come home to each other, we come home as the individuals God created us to be. Stephaine doesn't need Bishop Walker at home, and Joseph doesn't need Dr. Stephaine. We need each other. All couples of destiny need each other. And our hope is that you continue pursuing ever-deepening knowledge about each other so that your marriage is vibrant and exciting.

None of us ever arrive. Even the relationships and marriages we most admire have not arrived. We are always becoming. That's what becoming a couple of destiny is all about. It's about your willingness to begin a process of becoming. It's about walking through life with someone who challenges you, strengthens you, encourages you, holds you accountable, and brings out the best in you. It's about connecting with a person who is willing to accept you for who you really are and not what people think you should be.

## Talking Points

1. Join hands and pray for God to guide you and deepen your relationship.

2. Look in each other's eyes and say, "I love you. We are better together than we are alone."

3. Promise that you will say encouraging words to each other at least twice a day.

4. Commit to going three days without complaining about your spouse. If three days sounds too easy, try a week.

5. We are blessed by God to bless others. How are you blessing others in your daily living?

6. What is something new that you have learned about each other in the past month?

7. Share with your spouse how you envision your future destiny.

Chapter 2

# Becoming a Couple: Merging Two Worlds

When two people meet, they each bring their own worlds with them. These worlds are made up of such things as their unique histories, families, and beliefs. The more similarity—the more overlap—the easier it is for the worlds to come together. That is why it is easier for people with similar backgrounds and experiences to make it as a couple—there are just fewer differences to work through. But sometimes the differences are great; for example, one person, who may be successful herself, comes from a poor family with a single atheistic, alcoholic parent who does not value education, meets another person, no matter how successful, who comes from an affluent, aristocratic, teetotaling, church-going family who values education. With so many different values and perspectives, there is going to be a lot to negotiate. And their worlds, rather than merge, might just crash and burn.

Couples of destiny are no different. More similar backgrounds make merging the worlds of the individuals into the one world of the couple easier. But easier does not mean healthier or better. Just because a couple gets along does not mean that they are headed toward their God-given destiny. In our case, there were similarities but also some key differences in our worlds that would make for some funny stories later.

## Joseph's Story

Both Stephaine and I were apprehensive about how our worlds would merge. Stephaine is incredibly busy, and my schedule is insane. Medicine and ministry are two demanding fields to say the least. When we married, both of us were involved in community organizations and a variety of other things that competed for our time. But one thing we've experienced is that if something is of God, He will make it work. We learned that it's deeper than what you do; it's fundamentally about who you are. You've got to know that it's a process and that God will lead you and help you work together to make it work.

Think about your world and the world that your mate brought into your relationship. How similar were they? Do you come from similar family backgrounds? Do you have similar beliefs and values? Have you had some common types of experiences? Do you want the same things out of life? For most of us, there will be degrees of similarity and degrees of difference. Obviously, no two people are the same. But the question is, how do you address the differences? And how much of your individual world do you insist on taking with you into your new world as a couple?

### *Compromise, Compromise, Compromise*

Think of compromise as a promise coming together, a promise between the two of you blossoming into marriage. The first indication that our relationship would work was how easy it was for us to see each other on a regular basis. While she was in Boston and I in Nashville, there was not one weekend once we started dating that we didn't see each other. We discussed our calendar on the phone one day, and from that detailed discussion we put together a plan that would work for both of us. We literally chose to make it work. This is an area that many couples fail to realize. You have to make a deliberate choice to make things work in the relationship, but if our worlds were going to merge together there would be a need for compromise.

It's so important in relationships to understand that you are unique and that you have your own history. God has factored all this into the equation when He brings two people together and offers His promise of your destiny. But we often have to learn how to just coexist first. This is why it's important to be spiritual and see God as a part of the process of helping move your worlds together. You have to understand that when two people are in the process of becoming one, it is a spiritual evolution. You cannot do it alone; and you cannot do it overnight. Instead, you must allow God's hand to help you work on your relationship, help you have the spirit of compromise and patience. No wonder Paul mentions long-suffering in the job description of love in 1 Corinthians.

## *Shaped by What's Good for the Relationship*

I've seen so many couples refuse to compromise. Compromise is necessary if your relationship is going to mature and be what God intends. When we think of compromise, it should challenge us to look deep within ourselves at the significance and value of the relationship. Your willingness to compromise is one of the indications that you view the relationship as one worthy of longevity. When two people are willing to be shaped by the common good of the relationship, they give it life as they pour promise into it. Otherwise the relationship begins to perish.

Compromise speaks to a God kind of life: a life totally submitted to His will for you. And a relationship of destiny is one submitted to God's will. Remember, the devil desires to use your differences against you. He wants you to believe that there is no possibility that two people from two such different environments can come into a holy union—become one. God can do anything, and He works through yielded lives.

Stephaine and I had to submit to God's will personally in order for our life together to yield promise. I had to examine areas in my life that could potentially be hindrances to what God desired in our marriage. I tell couples that you can't rest the case solely on your point of view. Just because you are justified in a pattern of behavior doesn't mean it is always wise to continue in it. Compromise is necessary for the relationship's vitality and continued growth.

As the worlds of two people come closer, the process can present significant challenges. But if you are able to work through them with loving, faithful patience and compromise, your home can become a place of peace.

When God brought Stephaine and me together, it truly was a merger between the two worlds of medicine and ministry. As you know by now, she was and is a successful neonatologist, and I am a pastor of a large congregation. Our worlds couldn't be more different, yet we discovered that they were more alike than we had ever imagined.

### *My View of Stephaine's World*

When we first met, Stephaine was an assistant professor at Harvard Medical School, and when I visited "her world," as I vividly remember calling it, I was amazed. Medicine is a fascinating profession. Neonatologists operate in a unique silo. When they are in the hospital, they are in an intense environment. Working with sick babies is always difficult, yet I observed the tremendous care and attention the staff gave each one.

My first visit to the Neonatal Intensive Care Unit—the NICU—was with Stephaine. This was an opportunity for me to meet the folks who worked with Stephaine on a daily basis. I was simply blown away by the complexity of this profession. I knew she was brilliant, but walking in and seeing premature babies in incubators really made it clear that I wasn't with an average woman. It changed my perspective and helped me understand her world. I thought I knew, but going there really brought it home. I say this to make a point. It is very important to engage a person's work environment at least once early on in a relationship in order to have a comprehensive understanding of what drives your significant other for eight to ten hours a day. The time that we spend with our mates is usually after or before work, and you are better able to understand the impact that their job or career has on them once you've lived in it with them.

Healthcare is a tight-knit community of highly trained individuals focused on one goal—making the sick well. That is what that their world centers around. Stephaine explained to me that when she's on, she's on and when she's off, she's off. I didn't really understand what being "on" meant until I stepped in the NICU. The sweet and soft-spoken woman that I had come to know transformed in that place into a strong, directive-giving, no-nonsense professional at work. Her compassion for her patients is always evident; however, when she steps in the NICU, she has to call upon her skills and training and sometimes put her own preferences aside to meet the demands of that environment.

We all have demands on us from our environment. Perhaps your demands are from work, school, family obligations, or even friends. Has your spouse seen your environment firsthand? Are you different at home and at work? I once knew a manager of a large industrial plant. He was very successful there, in part because he never minced words; he was proactive and gave easy-to-follow orders. While this was a prescription for promotions and raises at work, he tried to run his home the same way. But, guess what, his wife and kids were not so keen about being ordered around in a no-nonsense tone. They resisted being ordered not to go to the school dance, not to borrow the car, and to fix meals the way he liked them. In his work environment, barking orders bred respect, but at home, it bred rebellion and disaster. The same responses to the demands at the job may not work in other parts of your world. But it helps for your spouse to understand why you are the way you are.

### *My World*

The world of ministry is equally demanding. My world is one of endless meetings, unexpected crises, study, deadlines, and intentional relationship-building. The church is its own world. The dynamics that exist within it are complicated, and churches have their own personalities. Before Stephaine and I met, my own church, Mount Zion, had become very protective of me. This was something that came about primarily because of the love they have for their pastor; however, after the loss of my first wife, they took on the responsibility of protecting me from the misguided intentions of others.

Churches that grow rapidly do so for a variety of reasons. One of those reasons is the charisma of the leader. This unfortunately creates personality-driven churches that depend heavily upon the pastor to be present at most functions. The pastor's presence usually contributes to the sustainability of the growth, thus placing great demands on him or her. We often refer to churches in this category as the "Jealous Mistress." They are called this because these churches demand all the pastor's time and energy. So here I was in my world, pastoring a mega-ministry to thousands, preaching every Sunday and Wednesday. I still preach seven times a week at Mount Zion, not including my travel schedule around the world. Meetings with members and key leaders and collaborating with folks in the community usually make up my week.

Now, I would have to figure out how to make Stephaine's world merge with mine. It looked impossible, but we soon discovered that God will give you the grace necessary to make things easier than they appear. Jesus said, "The things which are impossible with men are possible with God" (Luke 18:27). We are two professional people with two demanding worlds vying for us. But our worlds needed to merge if our relationship was going to have mileage.

When God spoke to Abraham about what His will was for his life, He already had the logistics worked out. So often in life we focus in on the how and forget the Who. I remember going for days, frustrated, trying to think how all of this was going to work. The flights, the scheduling, the uncertainties were just a few of the things that caused me anxiety. It was only when I prayed and asked God to handle it that it started coming together. There is a powerful song entitled "Let Go and Let God." This song continues to inspire me because it challenges us to release those things that are too big for us and allow God to be God. He can do a better job at managing it than we can. That's why the Scriptures say you should "[cast] all your care upon him; for he careth for you" (1 Peter 5:7). If this merger was going to work, we both had to trust God to do it.

****

## Stephaine's Story

### *No Soft Landing*

The ceremony was over, the wedding guests had all gone home, the dresses and tuxedos were all put away, and then there were two—the two of us, that is. I knew without a shadow of a doubt that my husband loved me. Every part of my being could and would testify to that. So that was never an issue. Our relationship up to this point had been fairly easy. We shared numerous things in common, from our basic values to our life philosophies to the way we handle our finances to our senses of humor, down to the type of cereal we ate (seriously!). We would frequently either finish each other's sentences or just look at each other and say, "Yeah, I know." That's how in sync we were. With all of that in common, and more, we knew we had it made! Early on, we were still on cloud nine, in wedding bliss central. Boy, were we floating—not a toe touching the ground. But when we did touch the ground, I have to admit, it wasn't exactly the soft landing I was expecting. I have since learned that many newlyweds experience hard landings. Perhaps it happened to you too, but this was new to me.

### *Some Background*

I had moved numerous times before. Actually, once I left home to go to college, due to education and medical training I never lived in any one place for more than three or four years. I obviously knew this move would be different, so I acknowledged that there was nothing that would adequately prepare me for the path I was about to take. Not only had I just gotten married but I had moved from the Northeast to the South, the Bible Belt—well, actually the BUCKLE of the Bible Belt—Nashville, Tennessee. Not a problem. I was actually looking forward to the change of pace. I was also starting a new job at Vanderbilt in their Children's Hospital. In addition, by virtue of marriage, I was now the First Lady of Mt. Zion Baptist Church, for which there is no real training.

Remember, I had gone to Mt. Zion in the mid-1990s, but back then it was a church of approximately 300 to 500 people—and growing, mind you. But, over the years since I left Nashville, it had grown to a congregation of well over 25,000. Now, also keep in mind that I had no close family or friends in the area either. When I say that every aspect of my life had changed, I mean EVERYTHING was new or different for me. Nevertheless, with the way that I approach life in general, I felt that it was not a big deal and that I could handle it and it would be no problem. Boy, did I have myself fooled.

## *A Furious Juggling Act*

For the first six weeks of our marriage, my husband and I were on tour for a new book he had just released. In that period of time, we may have been home for a total of about six or seven days. During the few days we were back in Nashville, we actually moved in to our new home, which had been under construction. When we finally arrived back in Nashville for a small break after the tour was over, it was time for me to start work, which I did with excitement. Although it was a different hospital, the medicine was pretty much the same—so I saw this as my mini-comfort zone in the midst of the chaos. The folks at Vanderbilt were tremendously welcoming and overwhelmingly kind.

Meanwhile, I was attending a number of functions at church so that I could meet people and so that they could meet me as well. I was also unpacking the house and getting acclimated to being a wife to my husband. Did I forget to mention that although the book tour was over we were still traveling out of town once or twice a week for my husband's preaching engagements at other churches all over the country?

From the outside it may very well have looked like I was handling everything great, but the reality was that I was becoming more and more overwhelmed trying to acclimate to *my husband's* world and trying to fit myself, my career, and the other aspects of my life *into* it rather then merging my world *with* his. One person described it to me as attempting to drink out of a fire hose. I would have to say yes, that's exactly what it was like, and unfortunately, before long, I could feel myself choking and drowning. Not because I could not handle each thing on its own but because I was trying to juggle EVERYTHING all at once. It is true that you may be able to juggle in that manner for a little while, but sooner or later you will start to drop things. If you don't take notice, pause, and adjust, eventually your world may come crashing down. I was juggling furiously in front of a lot of people, and with patients, church members, family, friends, and a husband to care for, the stakes were very high.

Whenever I thought I had caught my breath, I would be introduced to something else, meanwhile still getting acclimated to what I had in hand. Our life was basically go, go... breathe, then go some more! I didn't really complain—at least not out loud. I was just trying to keep up and juggle things as they came my way. On the flip side, my husband had his busy schedule, and we were faced with trying to interject some time for just us but found it more and more difficult. Although we were together most of the time, because what we were doing was technically associated with "work" it felt like we were growing apart as opposed to closer together. We were both so busy that at times it seemed as if we had nothing else to give, not even to each other.

The longer this persisted and the wearier we found ourselves, the more reluctant I became to bring it up. I knew that God had blessed me with an amazing husband in Joseph and I didn't want to seem ungrateful to God (I know it sounds silly now, but it's true). I didn't want to offend Joseph, because this was how he operated before meeting me. I was tired; he was tired; and frankly, I just didn't want the little bit of precious time we did have together to be clouded by "none-sense," or so I thought it was at the time. So I didn't say anything—not verbally anyway. However, because I refused to allow my concerns to come out verbally, they began to manifest in other ways. I found myself becoming short with Joseph in conversation, less patient, less tolerant of things that would otherwise never bother me. Of course Joseph would ask what was wrong, but I wouldn't—and really couldn't—give him an answer, mainly because I didn't truly understand what we were going through. Before this, we had always been in a blissful relationship.

So when I finally realized what the root of the frustration was, I knew I just had to stop everything and regroup—and that's exactly what I did. It was a serious reality check for me. I thought I could be Superwoman, but there was no way we would survive this way. Our relationship was built on honesty and full disclosure; I had to get back to that place. So one night we were in the car driving home from an engagement, and I just started telling him the things I had experienced and felt during my transition to marriage and to life in Nashville.

I knew I just had to stop everything and regroup.

I found myself trying to explain to Joseph all of the pressure I was feeling to keep up, however self-imposed. I explained to him the very distinct differences in our adjustments to our new marriage. For him, the only things in his life that changed were that we were married and living together, which for any newlywed couple is huge. Otherwise, every day he was driving the same car to the same job to work with the same people, hanging out with his same friends, essentially resuming his same routine he had prior to the wedding. THAT was not my testimony. Nothing was the same—*everything* for me had changed: different job, different colleagues, no friends nearby, and a nonexistent routine. Not that I was complaining, because I was married to the man that God had hand-delivered to me. And although I was struggling, I would do it all over again. However, I knew Joseph had no idea what I was going through during our adjustment period, and in order for him to be supportive the way I know he wanted to be, I had to be honest about my struggles.

## *Not Your World but Ours*

In our conversation that day, I pointed out that he would frequently say things such as, "Well, in my world we do this or we do that," referring to the church and all things related, which translated into him and all things related to him, which ironically now meant me too. But that was part of the problem. He was trying to fit me into HIS WORLD. With that, I reminded him that we were married, which meant that it was no longer HIS world, nor was it MY world, but rather now it was OUR world. And together we needed to figure out what that looked like—not worrying about what others felt it looked like from the outside in but being concerned only with what it looked like from the inside out. It did not matter what others thought. The only thing that mattered was what God thought and what made sense to us and OUR new life together.

I told him that, because I felt so overwhelmed, I had decided to take a huge step backward and "start over," so to speak. I would focus on the most important things and then slowly layer on the responsibilities from other areas. I would first prioritize God, our marriage, and our home, without apology, and focus on getting those things in order. When that seemed a bit more settled, I would then share that focus with my career. Then I would layer on activities from the church and Joseph's travel schedule. After that I would find my niche in community involvement and eventually start to find local friends and hobbies to enjoy. You can think of it as carefully putting together a beautifully decorated seven-layer chocolate cake—one layer at a time, as opposed to what that same cake would look like if someone accidentally dropped it on the sidewalk: one big chaotic mess, which is exactly what life had been feeling like lately.

I have to say that I let it all out, tears and all, and you know what? Joseph embraced it all. He understood what he could and asked questions when he didn't understand. Ultimately, he listened and we talked. In that moment, I realized what it meant when people say that in marriage, your love continues to grow stronger daily. I loved him more in that moment than I did the day we got married—and I never thought that that would ever be possible, but it was real.

In the midst of all of the craziness, we almost forgot how much we loved each other. We've learned that we can never allow life to make us so busy that we forget to take care of, protect, and pour into our marriage and each other. We both looked at each other and our level of sheer exhaustion and promised to not make a habit out of the last six weeks. It was not an option. Yes, we work hard; yes, we have a busy, fast-paced lifestyle; but we have to be able to pause and pour into each other even in the midst of it all. When two very busy people come together, it's so easy, once all the celebration is over and real life starts to settle in, to just go and go and go, as if you are on autopilot.

### *We Bless Each Other*

One thing we had to consciously remind ourselves of was that we were and are each other's gift sent directly from God! Even though we are married, it does not mean that the "dating" and pouring into each other stops—quite the contrary. It really must become more intentional, more in the forefront of your mind, simply because of all of life's other distractions. When was the last time you went on a date with your spouse? Why not do something special that you both enjoy tonight? What is one thing you could do today that you know your spouse would like? Try surprising your mate with a favorite meal, favorite dessert, or favorite magazine.

We realized that we couldn't allow the things of life to consume us so much that we failed to honor what God had blessed us with: each other. I am Joseph's blessing. He is my blessing. We must always remember that, and most importantly our actions should reflect that. PERIOD. We also agreed that if we ever found ourselves in a place where we felt we still were having difficulty finding time to pour into each other, we would make sure that our marriage was top priority, second only to God, and we would make provisions to cut back on whatever was pulling at us. Can you set aside thirty minutes just to relax and have fun each week?

****

## COUPLES ARE CO-DISCIPLES OF JESUS

MOST COUPLES EXPERIENCE A let-down after marriage. The celebrations and showers are over and day-to-day life returns. For some couples, their relationship never makes the transition or survives the inevitable disappointments of married life not being what they thought it should be or ought to be. Sometimes the anger or hurt of not becoming one the way they thought it should happen never really heals. This also means that their worlds can never fully integrate.

Our worlds were quite different, yet we recognized that there were commonalities as well. We decided that as a couple our business is healing. Both of our careers involve interacting with people and advising them in critical situations. And we both regularly consult with families who have to make difficult decisions. It takes great passion to engage people at this level, and we both have a gift to do so. We genuinely like people. Although that's a simple statement, the implications are far-reaching in regard to our being together. The fact that we both deal with people day in and day out helped us better adapt to each other's worlds. It was not difficult to explain the burdens and joys of such encounters because we both experienced them daily in our respective careers.

Relationships of destiny need common experiences in order to make their one world materialize. One of the most powerful examples of this is how Jesus enlisted disciples to enter His world and follow Him. Jesus took ordinary men on an extraordinary journey that changed the world forever. In Matthew 4, as Jesus walks on the shore of the

Sea of Galilee, He finds men fishing. They are in their world, engaged in their profession. Jesus does not minimize what they are doing; rather, He affirms them in it. He assures them that if they follow Him, He will make them fishers of men. He does not discount fishing, but rather assures them that He will expand it. Jesus merged their world into His mission. He knew what they were good at and wanted to transform their strengths to the glory of God. This is the wonderful thing about God. He doesn't expect us to give up what we are good at doing; rather, He wants us to be available for expansion so that His will can manifest in our lives. The only requirement is to follow Him.

The transformation the disciples experienced only happened when they submitted themselves to Jesus. Only when you obey Him will you experience a relationship of destiny. But Jesus does not bark orders. He leads by enticing you and luring your worlds into oneness with Him. And you can be sure that He only wants what is best for you. God merged our careers in such a way that we better impact the world for His glory. But we both had to be open for expansion and transformation so that this would happen. We could stay in the boat of our reality and neglect Jesus' voice to follow Him, or we could heed the call and experience His desire for our life.

Perhaps you are like the disciples—you are in your boat, doing what you know to do. By reading this book, God is speaking to you, calling you forth into greater things. You and your mate are being challenged to merge your gifts for a greater call. That's destiny. That's where God is glorified.

### THE RIGHT TIME IS GOD'S TIME

As we prepared for our careers, God was at work in our lives. Examine the parallels. We both understand long hours. We both understand how to change plans in the moment of crisis. We both understand the need for extreme focus, because the lives of others are in our hands. We both understand the power of prayer to get us through. These are just a few things that were working together for the good. The entire time, God was preparing one of us for ministry and the other for medicine. He was simultaneously preparing us for each other.

At this very moment, perhaps God is at work preparing somebody you haven't even met for you and you for them. If you walk in your purpose and allow yourself to be available to transformation, God will connect you at the right time and the right place. He will help your worlds come together in unexpected, mind-blowing ways. It can happen to you, because it happened to us.

## Talking Points

1. Think about what has happened to you and to your marriage this past year. What stress are you experiencing?

2. Memorize Romans 8:28: "And we know that all things work together for good to them that love God, to them who are the called according to his purpose."

3. Talk to your mate about how God is giving you patience to look for God's timing in your situation.

4. Talk about the adjustments you had to make or are making to merge your worlds. What are the differences in your worlds? What are the similarities?

5. Where do your worlds still need to merge to become "our" world? What does it mean that you need to change? Are you willing to compromise to strengthen your relationship?

6. What are some things you cannot or will not compromise? Is compromising sometimes OK?

## Chapter 3

# Not *His* Way or *Her* Way but *Our* Way

God loves us and plans for us. As couples seeking destiny, we know that God wants to give us the desires of our heart, but we must also attune our heart with God's. And what are the desires of God's heart? They are that we love and serve one another as Jesus Christ loved and served us. However, sometimes we miss the full meaning of God's love for us: love is not simply something that we feel; it is also about how we treat each other. This idea is true in the Old Testament, and then the New Testament takes it a step further. For Jesus, love means that a person is willing to lay down his or her life for another. John 15:12-13 says, "This is my commandment, That ye love one another, as I have loved you. Greater love hath no man than this, that a man lay down his life for his friends." In the context of a marriage, this means that each is willing to put the other person first, even if it comes at personal expense. If each of you lives this way, you will forge your way *together* toward destiny. It will not be *my* way but *our* way, just as it is not *my* relationship but *our* relationship.

As said in the previous chapter, even prior to two individuals coming together, God has already factored in who we are as unique people into the equation. And although two people can be extremely happy together, no one is exempt from the conflict of wanting things *my* way. Admittedly, Stephaine and I both have very strong personalities. We both rest the case on our point of view, and a lot of the conflicts we have had in our relationship have been because we both are quite passionate about our own way of doing things. Because this is so significant for couples of destiny, we have chosen to be transparent about our struggles in an attempt to help others work through their own conflicts.

## Joseph's Story

If you are going to be a couple of destiny, you cannot allow Satan to use pride to get in the way. Men have huge egos, and I've always viewed *ego* as standing for "Easing God Out." It may begin simply with how we clean up or when to clean up. When you are determined to have things your way, even small things can evolve into large-scale problems. Stephaine is a strong woman, and there is absolutely nothing wrong with that. She is quite successful in her life. And I had to realize that for most of her adult life she had been on her own, working in school, and independently managing the affairs of her life.

I also had my way of doing things. As a pastor, I had my rhythm down. My staff understood my cadence, and everybody who was close to me knew it as well. I knew how I liked my house to be. I am a very neat person. I am a very timely person. If I need to be ready at 6 o'clock, I am ready at 6. Before we married, I had my way of existing, and I was very comfortable with that. I enjoy playing basketball at 5:30 in the morning three times a week, as well as taking trips with the guys from time to time to just relax and debrief.

### *Not Lazy, Just Not an Early Morning Person*

I am and have always been an active person. I usually get up at 5:00 a.m. every morning and go through a routine to get my day started. Though I am a morning person, Stephaine is not. Though she is just as active, her activity must begin after 8:00 a.m. The compromise for us now is that when I schedule things for both of us, I make sure I don't do it too early. When we work out together, we make sure it's a time when she is at maximum capacity. She is not lazy; she is just not an early riser. Clearly she is quite productive, considering her amazing accomplishments. I have to give up my way and understand that that's the way her world is. In order for her to be productive and focused, she needs to sleep a little longer. I, on the other hand, can operate on four to six hours of sleep every day. Likewise, she has come to understand that I am my most productive early in the morning, so she knows that if there is something I need to do, she can let me know the night before because I'll be up early the next day to do it. Being unselfish is really all about healthy compromise and learning to embrace each other's needs.

### *Get Ready to Be Transformed*

As you can imagine, before we got married we were set in our ways. This is not something uncommon to any couple seeking to move toward destiny. As I mentioned earlier, transforming *my* way into a way for *us* is important if the relationship is going to survive. Paul tells us to be "transformed by the renewing of your mind, that ye may prove what is that good, and acceptable, and perfect will of God" (Romans 12:2). What a transformed mind does is seek the highest good for the relationship. It's not selfish; nor is it prideful. But sometimes we get the better of ourselves or we forget and just insist that *my* way is best, at the expense of the relationship. That's the time when your mate needs to help keep you accountable with a gentle reminder that there are two of you, and you both share in the relationship. Sometimes it's not about who's right; it's about what's right for the relationship.

Stephaine and I are not immune to wanting things our own way, but sometimes we just take for granted that *my way is the only way*. In this story, *my* way just sneaked up on us. Stephaine was raised in California and I in Louisiana. That may not seem like much, but some of our understandings were completely different. It's not that one was right or wrong; rather it was just the way we were raised. I remember being at her pastor's home in Boston after service for a dinner. This was a huge revelation of how different our worlds were. Looking back on it now, it's comical, but it wasn't when I first experienced it. In Louisiana, my parents raised my siblings and me a certain way. The boys in the house took care of the outside of the house, and the girls took care of the inside. When it came time to eat, the wives prepared their husbands' plates. That's what I grew up with in Louisiana. On the other hand, Stephaine grew up on the West Coast in a home where her father cooked and served the meal to the entire family.

Can you imagine the collision on the way? I'm sitting at her pastor's house after church. After we pray, I sit down assuming Stephaine is going to ask me what I want on my plate. She got her plate and commenced going through the line placing food on it without asking me what I wanted. I just sat hoping that eventually she would ask me what I wanted. When it didn't come and instead I received a question of when I was going to fix my plate, I was stunned into reality. As funny as that is now, it was the beginning of a process of intentional merging of our different backgrounds into our new reality.

### *Creating Our Way*

Another way persons try to get their own way is by trying to change the other person into what they think he or she should be. Forcing your mate into your mold is unhealthy to say the least, because it shows that you don't respect the other person and that you think of them only as an extension of yourself. Differences are healthy, but you have to learn how to make those differences your strengths, not your weaknesses, as a couple. You have to find a way for your differences to add value to your relationship.

Stephaine and I differ on a lot of things, yet we've learned to develop strategies that make it work for us. What it means is that I have to be willing to sacrifice some things for the relationship. Many couples miss this simple principle and wonder why their relationship never works.

Let's say that you enjoy sports and your mate doesn't but enjoys time in the bookstore. A good compromise would be going to the bookstore with your mate and reading sports magazines. Consider going to a sporting event and stopping by the bookstore for coffee afterward just to debrief. It's about finding what works for both of you and making it happen.

It may not be as complicated as you might think, but if you want to find a compromise, you will. But compromise does not mean that you get everything you want or even some of what you want *sometimes*. And it doesn't mean you have to do it that way forever, but it does mean that each of you takes turns giving and taking in the relationship. Sometimes there must be a departure from your way of doing things, even if you were raised a certain way and have done it that same way your whole life. When Stephaine talks about compromises later in the chapter, you'll see how we worked things out.

One of the things the devil loves to do is manipulate a person's emotions into feeling that *my* way is the only way or that there is no way to have it *our* way. I remember on numerous occasions early in our relationship where the enemy tried to plant seeds, telling us that finding our way would be too difficult for us to overcome. The devil will tell you things like "You can't live with someone like this," or "They are trying to change you from who you really are." You've got to cast down imaginations and every high thing that exalts itself against the knowledge of God. Remember, prior to your meeting there were years of experiences that created the person you are with now.

Those experiences helped shape our mates into who they are. Their way of solving problems, managing everyday life, and simply living was established as a system for survival for them. The same is true for you. When two people come together, they must understand the miracle of two becoming one. It's a spiritual thing, and it requires incredible fortitude and focus to make it happen.

What you will discover in developing a new way of existing in the relationship beyond your way is that it is quite refreshing. You will learn things about yourself that you didn't know. If it had not been for Stephaine, I would never have learned to ski, because I'd never been and didn't think I would like it—until I tried it. There are numerous things I do that Stephaine would have never done on her own, but now she has come to love and appreciate them. That's what relationships of destiny are designed to do. They add value. They create opportunities for greater exposure to new things.

## *Anointed for Our Assignment*

Once we find *our* way, we can be open to receiving *our* assignment from God. Again, Jesus shows the way. When Jesus leaves the Passover with His disciples, He heads to the Garden of Gethsemane. It was in this garden that heavenly business would be transacted. What Jesus teaches us is how to move beyond our way of doing things and pursue God's way for our lives. Jesus was sent into the world with an assignment. That assignment was to die on the cross for all of our sins. It would not be an easy task. Historically, Gethsemane was a place where they crushed olives for oil. It was truly a place of crushing. Out of our crushing, Stephaine and I came to realize that our assignment was all about healing. Healing in different ways, but healing nonetheless.

One of the things I share with people is that the anointing of God is the presence and power of God upon our lives. When God anoints you, He always anoints you for an assignment. There is a specific assignment associated with that anointing. The greater the assignment, the greater the anointing must be. The more immersed you are in living your destiny, the more open you will be to receiving what God wants you to do. Stephaine was assigned to my life, and I was assigned to hers. In order for the anointing to manifest in our lives, we both had to be crushed to rid us of our selfishness. If you find yourself struggling to move beyond your way of doing things, you are at the beginning stages of being crushed for a purpose greater than your own; because, ultimately, even *our way has to become God's way*.

When God anoints you, He always anoints you for an assignment.

Jesus prayed in the garden with His disciples. He took eleven of them with Him. He left eight at the gate and took Peter, James, and John further. When He prayed, He asked His Father, "Let this cup pass from me" (Matthew 26:39). In a real sense, He was asking for another way to do it. He was not trying to avoid it but simply negotiating another way to accomplish the same thing. How many times have you and I done this? "Lord, I'll do it, just show me another way to make it happen." Jesus' next statement is powerful. "Nevertheless not as I will, but as thou wilt" (Matthew 26:39). This statement is piercing. It challenges us all to examine how we hold on to our positions without regard to the will of God. Jesus kept His human emotions in check, and He teaches us how to transcend to the higher good. When you and I enter into relationships of destiny, we must also declare, "Not my will, but Thy will be done." We must seek God's will in every area of our lives.

Stephaine and I both live submitted to God's will. We recognize the importance of submitting our way of doing things to what God's intent is for us both. It requires constant prayer. Even as strong-headed as Stephaine and I are, God gives us the grace to work through our selfishness in order to find a new system. With His will as our guide, we now pray, "Lord, whatever your will is for our relationship, we are willing to do."

One of the things Stephaine and I discovered is that when we were set on holding our positions without working toward finding *our* way, our conversations were like tennis matches. We went back and forth, attempting to make our point and score. Sometimes the volleying would escalate to overhead smashes with exclamation marks. When we found ourselves communicating like this, we knew something was not right. If you find yourself "playing tennis," trying to score points without coming up with a system that works for both of you, you are moving in the wrong direction. Let your arguments and disagreements serve to remind you that you have an issue to work out. Let the pain of those times signal you to take a step back and call a time-out until the emotions cool and reason can prevail.

But sometimes, we just have to stop and laugh at ourselves. We both have to confess that, while volleying back and forth can be fun, it isn't the best way to work out a problem. What do you fight over? For most couples, it is money. Do your disagreements actually help you solve the issue at hand? Is there a pattern to your arguments? Do you fight fair? Does one person win most of the time? Does either of you keep score? Does one of you give in prematurely and then get back at the other later? Are you afraid that one of you might lose control and strike out in an inappropriate way? But if you can never resolve differences, or if things easily get out of control, you might consider talking to a counselor or to your pastor.

****

## Stephaine's Story

### *Unrealistic Expectations*

Despite the fact that I knew his family and he knew mine and we talked incessantly about our respective upbringings and childhood experiences, we soon realized that nothing can truly prepare you for living together as husband and wife. Once married, the reality of the fact that we had spent virtually our entire courtship in a long-distance relationship—with him in Nashville and me in Boston and a very conscious decision to not live together prior to marriage—began to settle in. Once we were finally married, and ALONE, slowly the differences in upbringing began to emerge.

The temptation is always to do things the way you've been doing them and simply try your hardest to convince the other person that your way is the right way. Sounds easy enough, right? Not so fast. Because, simultaneously, the other person is trying to convince you that not your way but THEIR way is the best way, and ultimately you only clash. Sometimes you even start to ask yourself, "Who is this person?" Is this the same person I married? Well, of course it is. When you were courting, because you were so "in love" and caught in the bliss, you both tended to just compromise and do whatever you thought the other person wanted you to do because, of course, you just want to make the other person happy. But when people get married, we bring with us our own set of unspoken expectations. Sometime these can be huge issues that should clearly be discussed prior to marriage, things like financial expectations and goals; career goals and expectations; number of children, if any; and how to handle those aspects of the relationship that are most important to you. These can also be smaller issues: where you will spend the holidays; who will cook; and who will clean.

Joseph and I thought we did an amazing job communicating our values, desires, and expectations, and I would still argue that we did do a great job. We talked about all of these things and more. We also talked about those things throughout our adulthood that could possibly impact our relationship; however, we underestimated how our respective childhood environments ingrained certain expectations in us that clearly influenced our views on the roles of men and women in marriage.

Honestly, I do remember actually having a very detailed conversation early in our courting about what we felt the roles of men and women were in marriage, and it was clear that we had some differences—Joseph's being very traditional, having grown up in the South and being a man of the clergy; my views being somewhat more liberal, having been a young woman who had spent my childhood on the West Coast yet lived most of my adulthood in the northeast and had been fairly independent and making a great living for myself. I recall him saying in one of our early conversations that he wanted a "domestic wife." I kindly replied by asking him what he meant by that, because it sounded to me like he wanted a pet. We went on to debate the traditional roles of men and women, and I revealed my less traditional views. After hearing each other, we eventually met somewhere in the middle. It seemed, though, that once we got married, everything we had previously discussed went right out of the window, as if we both thought the other was "just kidding" or something.

I can recall one of our early discussions (note I said "discussions" because we rarely argued—our disagreements were more like "heated debates"). As Joseph mentioned earlier in this chapter, we were at a barbecue at my pastor's house that moved indoors because of the rain. My pastor's wife and daughters were virtually finished cooking when we arrived. It was very informal. They had the food set out on the kitchen table, and when they said it was time to eat, everyone stopped doing whatever they were doing and walked over to the table. When Joseph and I walked up to the table, I picked up an empty plate and handed it to him, then picked up a plate for myself. We walked around the table together, basically serving each other depending on which dish was closest to us. Made sense to me! No issues here. Little did I know, Joseph was boiling on the inside. When we returned home, Joseph was really upset, but I couldn't understand why. He later told me that it bothered him that when we were at my pastor's house I did not make his plate of food for him.

In his attempt to get me to understand his frustration, he later revealed that he felt as if I was purposely disrespecting him in front of his colleagues. Naturally, I explained that that was the last thing I would ever do and had to give him a crash course in "Hale Household 101." (Hale is my maiden name.) Now, depending on where you are from, you may or may not be able to relate. Bottom line is that you have to understand that, for me, this was completely out of left field. I grew up in Los Angeles. In our home, the men—my father, my brothers, my brothers-in-law—did most of the cooking (not all, but most). For whatever reason, my mom and sisters all married men who could cook very well. As a result, the men cooked these amazing meals, then prepared and served the women's plates. It's just what I saw. It's all that I knew. I never gave it a second thought. HOWEVER, in my husband's family—it was the COMPLETE opposite.

In my husband's family, it was the complete opposite.

The women did ALL of the cooking and the men . . . well, they did not. The women cooked, served, made sure the men were fed, then ate themselves and cleaned up afterward. I knew this, but I didn't realize he had automatically transferred those expectations onto me.

### *"Aha" Moments*

For the both of us, this was a huge "aha" moment. In that moment, we realized that despite all of the talking, planning, and explaining we did prior to getting married, we were still holding on to a number of unspoken expectations. So we decided to try to just be honest with each other and ourselves, to sit and identify them, both large and small. For example, Joseph expected the wife to clean off the table after a meal, no matter what. I expected him to clean up after himself, because to me it made sense that if you use it, you can clean it. Growing up as a child, in our house everyone participated in clearing the table, except for the person who cooked the meal. As a thank-you for cooking, that person was exempt from cleaning. Not the case in Joseph's childhood home.

Based on his childhood experience, he expected me, his wife, to get up to cook breakfast every morning no matter what my schedule was and no matter what time he woke up. Did I mention that I am a physician who sometimes has to spend the night in the hospital to be on call and can sometimes be up for 34-36 hours straight without sleep, only to come home completely exhausted? I'm certain, then, that I also failed to mention to you that I am NOT a morning person, and that my husband chooses to get up at 4:45 a.m. at least three days a week to go play basketball at the gym with a group of friends. Who CHOOSES to get up at 4:45 a.m. if they don't have to?

All this to say, we had a great discussion! After a little back and forth about "whose way" we would adopt, we realized pretty quickly that the answer was NEITHER. We would not choose to do things the way his family did things, nor the way my family did things. Rather, we would figure out what would work best for us. Regarding the food serving situation, we decided that when we were in Shreveport, I would fix his plate for him simply because it was a family tradition there and to alleviate any questions about me and my dedication to my husband. You have to remember, I was new to the family and was still getting to know people; I personally didn't want to offend his family in any way. But most importantly, I agreed to do that because I love him and I don't mind serving him—he's my husband. It had just never dawned on me to do so. He agreed he would fix my plate when around my family, which, by the way, he never has had to do! It sounds silly, but it's true. We had to have a conversation and make a decision about it. Not because it was the most important problem in the world but rather because it was important enough that it even came up as a topic of discussion in our marriage. One thing we were acutely aware of and dedicated to was nipping issues in the bud while they were small, simple issues, versus ignoring them until they became huge elephants with the potential to destroy due to pent-up, unexpressed anger or frustration.

### *Doing What Works for Us*

In our home, we decided we would do whatever makes sense for the moment. Given how hectic our schedule is, whoever is free when it is time to eat fixes the plates and sets the table. If I am working in the hospital and he is at home, if he knows I've had a rough day, it is not unusual for dinner to be waiting on the table when I walk in the door. And I do the same for him. As far as cleaning up, in our house if you walk past it, you pick it up. You can't just leave your empty plate on the table if you are planning on walking past the sink—that doesn't make sense. At least empty the plate into the trash and take your plate to the sink. Whoever is not busy or exhausted is the one who cleans the dishes and puts them in the dishwasher. The truth is, however, usually, we both have crazy, hectic days, and those are the days we just lean on each other and work together to get food prepared for dinner and cleaned and put away fairly quickly afterward. It just makes sense to us.

As for breakfast, we decided that if you are up and you are hungry, you fix breakfast. Period. It's not complicated. What we have learned, though, is that we are very protective of each other, and we work very well as a team. So, for example, if I have to work a lot, and go in to the hospital early in the morning, Joseph will usually wake up when I do, fix breakfast, and pack a lunch for me while I get dressed, to help me get on my way because he knows that mornings can be—well, let's just say, challenging for me. Likewise, on Sundays, because Joseph preaches four services, I get up with him at "o'dark thirty" in order to make breakfast, help him get dressed and pack his briefcase, and make sure he leaves with a full spirit. Funny thing is, though, I no longer struggle to get up, and it doesn't feel like a chore, because I love him and I know he would do the same thing for me.

****

## FEELING GOOD ABOUT OUR WAY

IT WAS A GREAT FEAT TO COME to *our* way. *Our* way also sets boundaries on other relationships in our lives. It lets people know that we can no longer be engaged the exact same way we were when we were single. The expectations that people had of us as individuals can no longer exist with us as a couple. In a real sense, people who are very familiar with you will have to get to know you all over again. They must get to know the committed you. My friends now know that the Joseph who would in an instant jump on a plane and meet them in Vegas or New York to hang out, is not that same Joseph now. I have to check my calendar against my wife's and make sure that it works for us both. It doesn't mean that she has to go with me when I go; however, if there is something important going on in her life, I would hate to miss it.

## LET GOD BE OUR AIM

ULTIMATELY, GOD'S WAY IS OUR highest aim. His will is perfect and right for our lives. We have always known that our lives merged for a cause greater than our own. If our relationship was going to have sustainability, we knew we had to move beyond our own wills and submit to His.

You may recall the story of Jacob when he wrestled with God all night. Jacob had his own way of existing and was content in it. When God got ready to change Jacob, He sent an angel to wrestle with Him all night until he had to yield. Jacob's words are still powerful today: "I will not let thee go, except thou bless me" (Genesis 32:26). There is a tremendous blessing in this wrestling of wills. Ultimately, God will bless you and your relationship. Jacob was changed at that moment, and you will be as well.

## EFFECTIVE PRINCIPLES TO MAKE YOUR SYSTEM WORK

### *Confrontation*

Many of you may be curious to know how we make our system work. Here are some principles that we have found to be very effective. The first is confrontation. That word often has a negative connotation; however, it also can be a very positive word. In this instance we had a choice. We could have allowed some of these frustrating experiences to continue in our relationship, or we could confront them. To confront them meant we were taking them on, willing to examine our roles. When two people are seemingly stuck in their way of doing things, the natural response after arguing is to retreat. Retreating is not healthy, though, because it births numerous assumptions. We both choose to confront these head-on because we know they have the potential to threaten our relationship.

Perhaps you are reading this book and you've allowed your frustrations to come to a boiling point. If you find yourself at a place of retreat, it won't be long before you are at a place of resignation. God is giving you an opportunity to confront this issue in your relationship. Confrontation should not be a license to blame your mate for not seeing things your way. It is an opportunity to engage in the second principle: communication.

*Communication*

Once you've confronted an issue, it is time to have a serious conversation. And we are very intentional about talking things through. When we communicate, we eradicate assumptions and unrealistic expectations. When we come to an impasse, we choose to sit down and determine the cause of our feeling so strong about our way of doing things. One of the most powerful revelations we both discovered through communication was that it very seldom had to do with our point of view. We were holding on to our way of doing things because it was rooted in much deeper issues. For me, Joseph, it was feeling like I "was the man." For me, Stephaine, it was feeling "affirmed." Both of these were legitimate concerns, but they should never have caused such a barrier in our relationship. When we communicated, we were able to address the core issues rather than rely on assumptions.

What do you assume about your mate? He'll make a joke about whatever you're discussing, even if it's serious? She'll just go wild when you tell her something she may not want to hear? We all learn to "read" our spouse, but sometimes what we think is going on really isn't. Perhaps you say, "You told me this." But your mate says, "You may have said that, but what you meant was something else." Or perhaps you've said, "Don't use that tone of voice with me." And your mate says, "What tone of voice?" These are times that we need to clarify our assumptions. But clarity comes only through talking to each other.

### *Collaboration*

The third principle is collaboration. Collaboration is so important because it allows both of you to work toward a sensible solution. Remember, you must move beyond *your* way and develop *our* way. *Our way* is a system that governs the relationship. As the relationship evolves, boundaries are made clearer and other people have to respect those boundaries. We had to work through our own issues and decide on a way of existing within our relationship that would be ours. It was so important that we developed this because it helps us navigate through our marriage. We now have a phrase we use when it comes to our way of doing things. We call it "whatever is easiest." This means regardless of how we might individually think about how things should be done, we both submit to whatever is easiest. This provides for less stress in the relationship and gets things done efficiently.

As you consider these three areas of confrontation, communication, and collaboration, it is essential that you and your mate develop a system that works for you. We cannot emphasize this enough. We truly worked through this area and strongly believe you can as well. It's a process. It will not happen overnight. Your way of doing things is the result of a lifetime of experiences that now must be reconsidered so that you can coexist in destiny with the amazing person God has connected you to. God's will is always greater than your opinion or position. If you truly learn to "seek ye first the kingdom of God, and his righteousness," then "all these things shall be added unto you" (Matthew 6:33). There are so many things God will do in your life and your relationship when you adopt those three principles. Remember, yours is not an ordinary relationship. You are in a relationship of destiny.

## Talking Points

1. Talk about what you expected marriage to be when you first started dating. How does your marriage meet and not meet your expectations?

2. Discuss how your relationship is and is not different from those of your parents, grandparents, and other family members.

3. How has your relationship changed you?

4. What do you want in a marriage partner? What do you want in a husband? In a wife?

5. How do you divide up your responsibilities, and are you happy with it? Who does the household chores? Who has the final say about spending money or making investments? Who has primary responsibility for the children?

6. Name one way that "our" way is different from "his" or "her" way in your house.

## Chapter 4

# Check Your Baggage at the Door

The Scriptures teach us in Hebrews 12 that we should lay aside every weight and the sin that so easily besets us. If there is one area that prevents couples from experiencing the life God wants them to live, it is holding on to the past. Though the past is significant in terms of our formation, it should not paralyze us so that our destiny never comes to fruition. If you allow the past to influence your relationship, you will be guilty of making your mate pay for your mistakes and the mistakes of others. This is not fair and should never be the case.

When you become a couple, God blesses you with a unique person and a fresh start. Yes, there are lessons we learn from past relationships, but it's important that we don't become immobilized by the past so that we can't embrace the future. When Paul says, "press toward the mark" (Philippians 3:14), he implies that even your current relationship will have its own pressures and challenges. You don't need to add other folks' old challenges to the ones you already have in your new relationship. You must press toward the mark or destination with a spirit of renewal and possibility. Don't drag old issues into a fresh relationship. Check that baggage at the door. This was certainly true for us.

## Joseph's Story

Stephaine and I realized soon after we met that we would have to check some baggage. When I refer to baggage, I am referring to the fact that I had to deal with my grief over losing a spouse and to be careful not to put Stephaine in a position where she would be competing with my late wife's legacy. I also had to make sure that I didn't allow past relationships to skew my perspective of Stephaine. I also learned that Stephaine had baggage that she needed to relinquish. Her previous relationships were lengthy, and often she had invested much in them only to end up disappointed and hurt. She carried this pain deep inside, and from time to time it would manifest in our relationship. To her credit, she was able to get past trust issues; however, when anything happened in remotely the same way that it did in one of her past relationships, she would become emotional and express her concern that our relationship may not work out. Like me, she admitted that there were things influencing her, and then we were able to have candid conversations and move on. We made a decision to be intentional about checking our baggage at the door.

You will never realize the amazing potential that exists within your relationship if you allow past pain to creep in and suffocate what God desires to do within the both of you. I remember flying one day on a particular airline, and I had an extra bag. I was informed upon check-in that extra bags have a fee. Though I was allowed a set amount of baggage for my trip, if I chose to exceed that, it was expensive. When we exceed the luggage requirements for relationships, it can be costly and even cost us the relationship. Paul says in Philippians 3:13-14 that we must forget "those things which are behind, and...press toward the mark for the prize of the high calling of God in Christ Jesus." It's not that I have amnesia about what happened in my past. It just means that I refuse to empower those who have hurt me to now keep me from God's best for my life.

## *Going Forward by Looking Forward*

So many couples allow themselves to be crippled by past events in their lives. I once heard a powerful story about driving a car. In your car, you'll notice that there are two kinds of glasses with specific functions. The first is most obvious. It's the windshield. The second is the rearview mirror. The windshield is larger for a reason. It's designed for gazing. The rearview mirror is much smaller and designed for glancing. You cannot drive forward gazing through the rearview mirror, or you will put your life and the lives of those in the vehicle with you in jeopardy. The same is true in life. You can't go forward toward destiny while looking too long in the rearview mirror.

If we keep looking to the past, we minimize what God wants to do for us now. Other people have moved on in their lives and yet we choose to hold on to painful memories. Perhaps you still suffer from the nickname you had as a kid. Perhaps you regret that you gave yourself away too soon sexually. All of us have someone in our past—someone who continues to dominate our thoughts and who continues to speak to us in the inner places of our emotions even though the relationship has ended. Today is your day to let go and move on with your life. Your relationship of destiny commands it.

### *Do You Ever Really Get Over It?*

Someone once asked me, "Do you ever really get over it?" That is a legitimate question. Although we put the pain behind us and try to move on, the memory of what happens often is triggered by certain events. The point here is not to allow those memories to negatively affect your current relationship. It's not fair. My response to that question is in the form of an analogy. Think about this for a second. A father and his daughter were riding in a car one day when a bee got into the car. The daughter began to panic because she was afraid she'd get stung. The father maintained his focus and, while driving, caught the bee in his hand. The daughter was amazed at how the father was able to multitask, and she was relieved that the bee had been contained. After a few moments, the father released the bee, and it began to swarm around the car again. The daughter immediately went into panic mode, but the father showed her his hand. He had allowed the bee to sting his hand, and then he reminded her that a bee only has one stinger. "Although it swarms, I've got the stinger. It can buzz around the car; it can even land on you, but it can't hurt you."

Over two thousand years ago, Jesus took the sting of sin in his hands on Calvary's cross, and now, death can't hurt us anymore. Equally, when we are in relationship with Him, those things that have historically hurt us are also in His hands; and we can be comforted by Him, reminding us that those things can no longer cause us harm. You might see the person who hurt you out one day, but it's just a buzz and a swarm because the sting you felt years ago is no longer there. That's the power of letting go and turning that baggage over to God.

One of the things that many couples miss is that dealing with baggage does not necessarily happen right away in a relationship. It took time to accumulate it, and it will take time to release yourself from it. It's truly a process. That's why it's so important for us to be patient with our mates and assure them that we are sensitive to their plight. But what if *you* have serious problems letting go? Many of us have seen the reality show *Hoarders*. This show depicts persons who have significant difficulty letting go of things they have collected over the years. Although there may be a lot of sentimental value attached to them, these items clutter up their lives. The things they choose to live with often cause great strain in their domestic relationships, threaten their own safety, or cause others to believe they might be a little crazy. Counselors are brought in to help folks examine the reasons they cannot part with their possessions, and often tears of emotion flow as persons attempt to find release.

This reality show unfortunately reflects the reality for so many people in significant relationships. We hoard issues from our past. These issues threaten our current relationships and cause people to make assumptions about us. Why can't we just let it go? I've come to the conclusion that people don't need our judgment; they need our understanding and permission to walk through the process of deliverance. If you find yourself forcing a person to move on or if you say careless words to that person, you are literally delaying the release process. No matter how difficult our experiences might have been, it will take some time to truly release ourselves from them.

People don't need our judgment; they need our understanding.

It is never easy to let go of the pain of past relationships. It's almost as if we hold on to the pain because it helps us keep the memory of the person alive—like we can somehow go back in time and have our relationship turn out differently. We often ask ourselves, "What if it had been different?" And we all know people who live their lives with "what if." What if she had not met so-and-so? What if I had done something different? What if we'd had more time, more money, more friends? What if I'd been smarter, richer, cuter, more athletic? If you dwell in the land of "what if," you don't have the time or energy to live in the now. Instead, what if you gave up living in the past and opened yourself to the good gifts God has waiting for you? What would you do with all that freedom God offers you? One way I found is to begin by acknowledging that you were not meant to be alone.

## *You Never Have to Walk Alone*

It is so important to ask God to help you with the pain and the memories. Don't try to do it yourself. He knows what you are struggling with, and He's able and willing to assist you. God did not connect you to a relationship of destiny for it to be tainted by negative past experiences. The book of Hebrews says that weight from the past easily besets us. It prevents us from truly knowing the person God has placed in our lives. It prevents us from opening up so that person can truly know us. It affects trust and transparency. No one deserves that.

Of course, past experiences are not always negative, but even positive past experiences can have an adverse effect on your current relationship. By this I mean to suggest that the positive things in your past relationships can be projected as expectations on your current relationship. Although you have positive memories, it is unfair to expect the person you are with now to compete with the person you were with in your past. This was so very true for me. I could not put Stephaine in a position where she had to compete with the legacy of my deceased wife, Diane. Diane was Diane, and Stephaine is Stephaine. Often, people make the mistake of comparing one relationship with another, so that the new person feels at a disadvantage. This is not a healthy thing to do in relationships. As I've said before, Stephaine could not marry Diane's husband. She needed to marry *her* husband. I need to give Stephaine an opportunity to love me in her unique way and not lay it side by side with how Diane treated me. If you desire your relationship to thrive, recognize the hold the past has on you, whether positive or negative, and then be willing to live in the now with the person God has given you.

### *Lay Your Burdens Down*

Hebrews 12:1 tells us to "lay aside every weight, and the sin which doth so easily beset us," he is not suggesting that we can't run the race but saying that we would run much better if we laid the weight aside. Excess baggage slows us down and delays our destiny. Can you imagine who you will be when you release this pain from your life? Can you imagine how different you will be when you truly let go?

### *Sometimes Baggage Just Appears*

After the wedding, when Stephaine and I moved into our home, I had a surprise regarding my own personal baggage. I didn't realize the number of things I had brought from my first marriage into our new house. When Diane passed away, I made it a point to keep specific pieces of art that were meaningful to her. Although I had given many other items to family members, these items followed me to this new home. I never thought of their impact while I was single. They were just pieces of art that reminded me of that season of my life. I would pass by them and laugh or have deep thoughts about my past with Diane.

When we moved in, this became a very delicate issue for us. To her credit, it took Stephaine a while to bring it up, because she never wanted me to feel that she devalued

Diane's legacy. She has proven her commitment to the preservation of that legacy, but I knew that something was wrong when we were just walking around the house and she began asking about certain pieces. When I mentioned where they were from and the story behind them, I could see a struggle in her eyes. I had been oblivious to the fact that I carried this baggage into my new marriage. Even Jesus reminds us that we can't put new wine into old wineskins. Here I was expecting Stephaine to be comfortable with items in our new home that came from my marriage to Diane and my old life. When we discussed it, I began to see how this affected her and immediately we began to make some useful decisions. She did not ask me to throw the items away, nor would I, but I was able to relocate them with family members so that they could be appreciated and my marriage could have the fresh start it needed. Stephaine and I have since begun our own collection that speaks to our life together. It was so important to have this discussion, because I had no idea that I was carrying that baggage. It just showed up.

I distinctly remember another occasion when it was clear that Stephaine and I both let go of some baggage. We had a huge disagreement that revealed deeper issues for us both. When it was clear we were holding on to issues in our past that had nothing to do with each other, we had a moment of confession. I say this because it's so important to be honest with your mate about your baggage. We both owned our baggage and explained to the other how it had affected us over the years. I realized that I had been haunted and taunted by those issues, and I had made the terrible mistake of suppressing them. It's easy to suppress what you don't want to deal with. This is how the devil gets a foothold into so many relationships. We act without realizing that something gives rise to the action. Once we are willing to investigate what gives rise to the action, we then are able to address it. We both were very clear that we needed to help each other move past those issues.

What baggage are you carrying? Is it interfering with your current relationship? Are you ready to free yourself of the past and move on? Moving on does not mean that you forget your past, but it does mean that your past no longer controls you. And it also means that you are free to enter into your new relationship and to learn new ways—maybe better ways.

****

## Stephaine's Story

Prior to getting married, as a single young woman throughout undergraduate school and my medical training, I had the opportunity to live in a number of places—Nashville, New York City, Philadelphia, Los Angeles, and Boston. Needless to say, while waiting for God to bring Joseph into my life, I had my share of dating opportunities. Many of them left me emotionally bruised or scarred. This often resulted from dishonesty, infidelity, or emotionally abusive personalities due to either people's insecurity or their own familial generational curses. Amazingly, though, I never grew bitter toward the idea of one day finding true love. I refused to let the behavior of others make me bitter or hateful and in turn risk missing out on my blessing that God had already declared would be for me one day.

We've all heard news or read articles quoting statistics of the ratios of single women to single men or the reports on the probability of getting married after a certain age. When I would come across this information, I would simply go back to the promise that God made me. I knew what I had asked God for. Although others around me at times allowed the data to discourage them, I knew that, as long as those numbers of single men were still in the thousands, I was good! Because I required only one. It makes me laugh to think of how we rationalize at times. But honestly, looking back, I was able to continue to move forward because I wholeheartedly believed that God would stand firm on His promises and present me to the soul mate he had set aside for me one day. All I had to do was be patient.

## *Not **If** but **When***

In relationships as well as in other areas of life, I firmly believe that what's for you is for you. No one, not even the devil, can take those things away. Instead, he simply tries to discourage you with obstacles and challenges in hopes that you will give up on your own, causing you to miss the blessing that God has already set aside for you. To me that's like giving up near the end of the twenty-fifth mile of a twenty-six-mile marathon, all because it's getting painful and the end is nowhere in sight—only to realize later that if you had hung in there, the finish line was literally just right around the corner. Because you can't see the end, you get discouraged. Perhaps a building or a tree is the only thing blocking your view, but not being able to see it doesn't mean that the promise is not near. If God said it, then I believe it and consider it done. Although it may take a while to manifest, I understand that when it comes to God's promises, it's never about IF but rather WHEN.

Obviously, I had no idea that when God decided to reveal my blessing it would be someone as amazing as my husband, Joseph. Never in a million years would I have thought that I had that kind of favor on my life. I did, however, know that God would not allow me to go through what I went through in order to leave me bruised and not bless me with the desires of my heart. I also had the wherewithal to thank God in the midst of my journey, because I recognized that with every experience comes a lesson. You learn what you want and don't want, what you will tolerate and will not tolerate. You learn what qualities your ideal mate needs to possess and what the deal-breakers are. You also mature and grow stronger and wiser in the process because it certainly is that—a process. One thing for sure, after all was said and done, at the very least I knew that I had learned quite well what love DID NOT look like—and that in itself is a gift.

Although I said I did not grow bitter, admittedly I did slowly grow distrustful and guarded when it came to letting strangers near my heart. As a result, when I first met Joseph, I was only "cautiously optimistic." I'd been let down so many times in the past that I just did not want to get my hopes up only to end up face-down in the dust. In our very early conversations, I found myself listening intently to see if he said something that contradicted one of his previous statements. I was really checking to see if he was truthful and a person of high integrity. And of course, with time, I realized that indeed he was. He has an impeccable sense of integrity. Is he perfect? No, of course not, but neither am I. But he always does what he says he's going to do. Even to this day, he has never made a promise to me that he hasn't kept. He practices what he preaches. What he expects others to do, he does—he leads by example. That, to me, speaks to integrity.

I distinctly remember another conversation Joseph and I had about our past relationships prior to getting married. I was very candid about my experiences and the effects I thought they had on me, both good and bad. I remember saying and truly believing that I could easily leave the past in the past given the fact that I now knew Joseph, and he was so different. He is loving, respectful, and supportive, and as I said before he has an amazing sense of integrity. Ultimately, I knew that no matter what, he would always stand beside me, protect me, and have my back. I felt I was good, done, over the past! But it was Joseph who told me that erasing the effects of the past is easier said than done. He knew it would be a process, not an event. But even with that he vowed to always stand with me and allow me to go through that

> He will stand beside me, protect me, and have my back.

process. I, on the other hand, felt that I was allowing the past to defeat me or dictate things in my life if I thought about or reflected on things for any significant length of time. I knew that in no way did I want the past to impact my future marriage. After our conversation, I tried to simply bury everything and put it to rest. Little did I know that some of the issues of the past that I "put to rest" had never truly been worked out in my spirit as I had assumed.

### *The Importance of Trust*

It wasn't until after we were actually married that I began to see little hints of the past start to creep up. The transition to marriage with someone who, if need be, was more than capable of truly taking care of me, our home, and our family—not just financially but also as a leader in the home as a man—was a tough one for me. You might think that sounds really strange and it SHOULD sound strange. Most of my previous relationships were with people who, over time, I discovered I could NOT rely on to do any of the above. They would say they were going to do things and time would pass only to reveal that nothing had been done, and I would be left high and dry. Or they would make numerous empty promises that left me feeling like I couldn't rely on other people. So it just got to a point where I would take over and do everything myself, because I felt like I couldn't trust others to do what they said they would do.

A few had issues with managing their finances, holding down jobs, or making sound or wise decisions in other important areas of their lives. You may be thinking, well, how did you ever get involved with people like that in the first place? I can say that at the time I was very trusting of people and had a tendency to believe that, in general, people were really good at heart, so I would always give others the benefit of the doubt. I mean, after all, why would someone lie to me? Right? Although clearly I was young and VERY naïve, I accept full responsibility for not just being in but often staying in dysfunctional relationships. I found myself constantly giving others the benefit of the doubt, even when they did not deserve it. At some point I had to wake up to reality. People are who they show themselves to be. This is not always what you are hoping for, and sometimes, instead of accepting what you see, you make excuses and make the mistake of trying to "fix" them. Life is real—it's not Ken and Barbie. You cannot control or change other people. Only God can do that. Take it from me: this is not a healthy way to live your life. You must learn to realize that what you see is what you get. Period. Move on.

Now don't get me wrong here. It is important that as an aside I say that a marriage or a mate should not be defined by a person's finances, earning potential, or what someone can *do* for you. I'm not saying that at all. There are a number of other amazing qualities and characteristics that are just as important, maybe more so. But, having said that, if someone has poor credit or a history of poor financial management, I see it as a window into that person's character and integrity. Purchasing what you cannot afford in an attempt to impress people who don't know you, trying to keep up with the Joneses by spending yourself into a debt crisis, not repaying people or companies when you say you will, not being able to negotiate basic interactive skills in order to keep a steady job, making unwise financial investments—these all speak to a person's character and ability to make sound decisions. So it's not the fact that the person may have poor credit or be in significant non-education-related debt; rather, it's what it suggests that's the issue. And, unfortunately, I allowed myself to be in relationships where I often felt used by people who were later found to have all or some combination of the above issues, which is why I feel more than comfortable and qualified speaking about it.

As a result of all of this baggage I carried around, early on in our marriage I found myself constantly checking in with Joseph to make sure he did what he said he was going to do. For a portion of our bills, I set up automatic bill payments and would go through the online banking statements at the time the bills were due to make sure there were no "additional" random expenses. Not that my husband didn't have impeccable financial credit like me, because he did! When he would tell me he would handle something, whether simple or complex, sadly I would follow behind him constantly checking, asking if things had been done, telling him how best to do them, or worst just taking over and doing it myself. All of this would frustrate him to the core. This behavior was such an ingrained part of me that at first I didn't even realize I was doing it. Joseph would look at me and say, "Baby, I'm your husband. I said I would do it; please just trust me to take care of it." Or he would remind me, "I'm a man. I will always hold it down in our marriage," meaning that he would always take care of everything and anything that needed to be taken care of and that I had nothing to worry about. But it took me a while to receive this, mainly because I simply wasn't used to this.

I recall another incident when it was very late in the evening and we had just gone to bed when suddenly his cell phone rang. Well, naturally, I sat straight up in the bed and just looked at him as if to say, who is that calling YOUR cell phone at this hour and aren't you going to answer it? My mind started racing a million miles a second. I started to get so upset. The devil sure was busy with my imagination. Needless to say, I felt foolish when it was the church hotline telling him that someone had been suddenly hospitalized! Can you imagine how silly I felt? It honestly frightened me how quickly past emotions rush to the forefront when we see anything that remotely resembles part of a negative experience of the past. I had to ask Joseph to forgive me for my response, because of course he had never given me any cause to think it would be anything improper. When you've been hurt or scarred in the past—whether it be by a friend, previous spouse, family member, or whomever—you have to be mindful of how that baggage may revisit you, and you must be cognizant to guard against those feelings creeping into your spirit.

### *Residual Baggage*

I was treating Joseph as if he was someone else—almost punishing him for other people's shortcomings or inabilities. That clearly was not fair. The fact that I had brought that type of residual baggage into our marriage frightened me and at the same time saddened me. The last thing I wanted my husband to think was that I did not trust him or that I did not believe him to be capable. I had to unlearn those habits and retrain my mind, because I had married an amazing man who I actually could rely on. I just didn't really know how to allow myself to. It took some time to get used to the fact that I truly had married a man of integrity in every sense of the word. It was another process, not an event, but he was very patient with me, and we worked at it together as a team.

### *Talking It Out and Through*

It was clearly divine intervention that, prior to getting married, Joseph and I talked openly about our past. We understood that truly knowing each other was also about knowing the experiences that made us who we are, both the good and the bad. So the night of the late phone call, after Joseph got off of the phone, when he looked at me and saw the horrified, apologetic look on my face, he already knew why I had responded the way I did initially. He knew it had nothing to do with him, although in that moment it was still a bit hurtful. Thank goodness today we can laugh about it, but that night it really wasn't all that funny.

It is imperative that you are honest with your spouse about your past experiences and the baggage you carry with you, because until you have thoroughly dealt with it, it will continue to resurface. Sometimes we may feel that everything is fine because we've pushed the memories to the back of our minds or have attempted to block them out somehow. That's what I did; I felt that since I was in a safe relationship with the man I was destined to be with that I could just pack everything away because none of those people mattered anymore. I was so wrong. You can't put significant past experiences in a box and expect them to take care of themselves and not resurface some way, somehow. At some point you have to deal with the issues of the past head-on, without fear, so that you can deconstruct them, eventually move on, and put them in their rightful places. I learned the hard way that, until they are dealt with, they are not going away.

### *It's a Process to Get There*

The other issue is that many people expect to be able to quickly deal with these feelings and issues, to have instant gratification, as if you can say "poof"—it's gone. This is not always the case either. Think about how long it took you to come to that place of frustration, anger, or distrust. It was a process to get there; it will be a process to come back. Together, both Joseph and I had our share of baggage, but because we were open and honest from the beginning, we understood the areas where we needed to be patient with each other, making it easier when possible to work together as a team to heal our wounds.

****

## CHECKING BAGGAGE AS A TEAM

GOD BROUGHT YOU TOGETHER to be a team. Romans 15:1 says, "We then that are strong ought to bear the infirmities of the weak." As a team, we encourage each other and sometimes we help carry each other's baggage. When one of us has a bad day and relapses into past issues, it is the other's responsibility to be strong so that we can move on together. Teams don't discourage each other, rather they encourage each other to do better. Spend time with your mate and assure him or her that you are willing to walk through the process together.

We have an understanding in our relationship. When baggage shows up, we refuse to allow it to threaten our marriage. We refuse to allow the devil to use our imaginations and take us places where we don't need to go. Just because people have to work through issues of the past does not mean they don't completely love you. We love each other so much that we deal with the baggage together as a team. The past is truly the past, but it did exist. You cannot go through life as though it didn't exist; however, you can disarm the past so that it won't have power over your current reality.

We challenge you to pray as a couple about the baggage in your life. Ask God to give each of you the grace to encourage the other as you deal with those painful realities in your past. Spend time in God's Word together. Know that God is willing and able to help you move beyond every hindrance and bring you to a place of complete wholeness. Remember that it's a process and it may take some time, but if you are willing to talk it through, you can do it. There are so many doors God has for you and your mate, but it's necessary that you check your baggage at the door.

## Talking Points

1. Tell your mate about how you were hurt in past relationships.

2. Do you keep your promises to each other? Do you believe that you can call on each other in an emergency for needed support and help? When was a time that you needed help and your spouse was there for you?

3. How is your teamwork? If you had a mascot, what would it be? How do you handle making decisions as a team? What are some good decisions you have made in the past?

4. Tell your mate three things that you love about him or her and why.

5. On a scale of one to ten (one being low and ten being high), how much do you trust each other? Why? Give an example.

6. What is your favorite way to demonstrate your love to your spouse?

Chapter 5

# Maintaining My Identity in "Us"

As two people come together as one, it almost seems taboo to talk about holding on to your own identity. After discussions about merger and oneness, it seems selfish to do so. But if relationships are going to be healthy, couples must not be afraid to maintain their personal identity within the relationship. We must share and be selfless—selfless not in the sense that we don't have a self, but just that we think of ourselves *less* and of our mate *more*. When you have committed yourself to getting to know each other, you bless the other person by sharing the "real you." Too often people portray themselves to others as someone other than who they are. Your identity is important, and you should not have to change who you are to be with the person God has for your life. Although there will always be compromises, to achieve true oneness, you also need to maintain your unique identity.

## YOU, ME, AND US

In order for your relationship to develop an identity, there must be a clear understanding of your individual identity within it. When people don't really know who you are, they run the risk of not fully appreciating what you bring to the table. The question is simple: are you maintaining who you are in the midst of it all, or have you lost *you*? When your identity is lost in the relationship, it creates disillusionment within the relationship. You begin to wonder if the other person truly values and appreciates you. If it continues, you might begin to question whether your mate knows you or not.

## YOU ARE FEARFULLY AND WONDERFULLY MADE

IN A COUPLE, THOSE TWO PEOPLE are drawn to each other. Part of that attraction is each other's identity. We grow and learn to accept certain things about each other and that, in itself, contributes to the health of a marriage, but we've all met people who approach relationships with a "messianic complex." These are people who feel it's their responsibility to change a person into who they think he or she should be. This is unhealthy in relationships and will cause serious problems within marriage. We are who we are, and we constantly change by the grace of God. God wants us to change through learning, growth, and enhancement—not through coercion. When God brought Eve to Adam, they both had to accept who they were individually in order for them to be who they were going to be together. God makes us individually unique. Psalm 139:14 says that we are "fearfully and wonderfully made." (The word "fear" as used here means "worthy of respect.") Our identity is important to who we are; it is something to be respected and held in high regard. And it's important to who we are as a couple. Life will change us and can cause us to alter our course toward destiny. Adjustments will have to be made. However, our expectation is not to be a different person but to be open to grow together in who "we" are. Make no mistake about it—we each grow every day. We are evolving and becoming what God wants us to be. None of us have arrived.

As you know, identity is shaped by experiences, which contribute to our perspectives, responses, and values. We are who we are, but we are not yet who we will be. When we enter into relationship with Jesus Christ, we are transformed and become who He has called us to be. This is the person God positions for relationship, but He does not position people who do not submit their lives to Him. Because God will not force us to change, we have to freely choose His path and His ways.

Freely choosing is important because, without Christ in your life, you will have a tendency to make your relationship an idol—something that tries to replace God at the center of your life. Idols tempt us not only to turn from God but also to lose ourselves in pursuing them. We all know people who have lost themselves while pursuing ungodly vices, but we can also lose ourselves by putting our mate on a pedestal—making our mate some kind of perfect being. We do this because *we need* them to be perfect, not because *they need* to be. We lose ourselves in them because we don't feel complete within ourselves and need someone or something to fill the void.

Losing yourself is especially tempting when you are lonely or have poor self-esteem. We've all seen people who faithfully prayed to God for a relationship, but once their prayer was answered, they did not seem like the same person anymore, because the relationship became so consuming that it snuffed out everything else—even love of God. Within the context of the relationship, you must see yourself bringing value and contributing to it. You cannot lose who you are in the process of propping up a relationship.

## Joseph's Story

When I think about who Stephaine is, I often think how her identity was the very thing that drew me to her. I've heard people say more than once that they have lost themselves in the process of trying to make a relationship work. Stephaine and I were very intentional about not losing who we are within the context of our relationship. We were determined to first embrace those things that make us uniquely us. Our fears, joys, challenges, and hopes are all important to embrace. But we had to communicate about these areas so that we would ensure that the other person genuinely knew us. I never wanted Stephaine to feel that she, as a unique person, was not important to the relationship.

### *Self-Realization*

There are a few things that you must do in order to ensure that you sustain your identity. The first thing is self-realization. What I mean here is that it is important to recognize who you are. You would be amazed how many people don't know who they are because they have allowed others to define them. People have spoken things over their lives, and as a consequence they have embodied only those words in their lives. If someone tells you all your life that you are unattractive and ignorant, you might begin to embody that in your daily walk. This contributes to low self-esteem.

There is a story in Mark 5 about a man possessed with demons. In verse 9 Jesus asks, "What is thy name?" The response of the demon within the man is, "My name is Legion: for we are many." Often we see the outward manifestation of a person's action, but we are unaware of the inward turmoil they experience. I've often wondered why people act the way they act in relationships, but this passage sheds tremendous light on the situation for me. *Legion.* There are layers of past issues and pain in folks' lives that cause them to live in ways inconsistent with who they really are. The devil's objective is for us to lose our identity in the dysfunction we have experienced.

It is important that you come to a point of self-realization and know who God made you to be. *It's not what people call you that makes you who you are; it's what you answer to.* If you don't embrace who God has called you to be, you will never be ready for a relationship of destiny, and you will allow yourself to be defined by the inconsistent perceptions people have of you. I've seen so many people fall prey to the callous statements of others regarding their destiny, thus destroying their self-confidence. You must be confident in who you are. That is one of the things that drew Stephaine and me together. A lack of confidence is usually the first indication that your identity is shaky. God is calling you to be confident in who you are in Him.

### *Relational Perspective*

After self-realization, the next thing to embrace is what I call a relational perspective. This means *you do not allow yourself to be defined* by the relationship, rather *you define it*. Whatever the relationship is to become is a result of the impact your identity will have upon it. Stephaine's unique personality contributes to the success of our relationship. My personality does the same. We often say that God put us together, because He knew that nobody else on the planet was ordained to be with us but us. That's how God works. He knows the person who has been ordained for us. This is the person who can accept us for who we are and grow with us in this journey toward destiny. No relationship will "fix" who you are, and you cannot "fix" another person by being in a relationship with that person. Your relationship will change you but will not remake you, and it will not become a substitute for who you are on the inside.

God always has a purpose in mind—His own perspective and vision when He brings two people together. The relationship is the vehicle He uses to bring His intention into being. Allow me to explain this further. Not long ago, I shared with some church leaders that vision is not building buildings. When a church identifies the building of a new church as the complete vision for that church, it misses the essence of what a vision is. The building is only a *strategy* to fulfill the vision. If you build a building without embracing the totality of the vision, you might build too small. When you know the vision, you plan the building in such a way that it supports the vision. The vision does not lose its identity within the building. The building does not subsume the vision but is supported by the building.

In the same way, when you see your relationship as a strategy to fulfill the vision, rather than the end result of the vision, you can begin to understand the significance of this principle. Often when we pray, we pray for the relationship as the end result of our prayers: "Lord, please bring somebody in my life." We should be praying, "Lord, please allow my life to give you glory." He then will connect you with a strategy, which may or may not be a relationship that can be a conduit to fulfill you with something beyond yourself. A relationship's purpose is to sustain and facilitate what God is going to do. You never want to downsize a vision because the building is too small. You also don't want to compromise your identity and enter into a relationship with someone who will interfere with the plans God has for you.

## *Can't Anybody Beat You Being You*

The next thing to remember is that part of our identity is tied up in social roles and titles. We all have them, whether we are a spouse, employee, citizen, or even Christian. When I look at the social context in which Stephaine and I exist, identity becomes a fascinating issue for us. Being a pastor is part of who I am, and within the church community, people often refer to the pastor's wife as First Lady. This title carries with it a great deal of respect, admiration, *and* expectation. Although it took Stephaine a while to accept the title, she finally did. The challenge for us has been to help people realize that she is a physician with a career of her own. Although she is the wife of Bishop Joseph Warren Walker III, she has an identity beyond that. Mount Zion has taken to affectionately referring to her as "Dr. Steph," which shows that they value her identity.

I remember ministering in a particular city and experiencing again the impact and importance of role expectations, but this time it was regarding my wife. As we arrived, the pastors' wives were in an office gathering. When Stephaine entered, she was immediately asked how long she had been in the ministry. Every pastor's wife in the room was in full-time ministry with their husbands and many were considered co-pastors. Stephaine's answer caught many of them off guard. She indicated that she was in ministry but not as they imagined. When she explained that her ministry was being a physician, it was clear that this was a new paradigm for many of them. I will never forget the conversation we had after that, because she felt so uncomfortable with what they perceived she should be and should do in her role as a pastor's wife. It was an awkward moment, but Stephaine met it with ease and grace—in part because she knows who she is and her identity is not consumed by being a pastor's wife.

When we were dating and talking about our future together, I remember sharing with Stephaine that it was important for her to be herself. It was important to me that she not fall into some ecclesiastical expectation. She feared that there was this blueprint that she needed to follow to be with me, so it was important to reassure her that she needed to first be my wife. Just as she fell in love with Joseph and got to know Bishop Walker, I fell in love with Stephaine, not First Lady Walker.

Remember to give your mate permission to be himself or herself. It is so important to value who people are and not allow social expectations to define who they should be. At the end of the day, you come home to a person—not to a role. After all the makeup is off and the suit and tie are back in the closet, you live with this person, who others may only think they know. My grandmother used to say, "Can't anybody beat you being you."

## *Giving Yourself Room*

One of the joys of our relationship is that I have room to be me all the time. There will be more about giving your mate space in a later chapter, but I just want to say here that, in our relationship, no pretending is necessary for either of us. Because we have come to know who the other is completely, it makes for some interesting dynamics socially. Often when we are in social settings, we communicate nonverbally, because we know what the other person is thinking. We've said on numerous occasions, "I know you didn't like this or that because I know you." As your relationship deepens, it is essential that your mate gets to know your identity apart from who others expect you to be. Your truest character is that which exists when nobody is around but you. The real you is who should be valued and protected within the context of the relationship. Who are you when no one else is around? Do you laugh more easily? Are you kind and loving? Are you honest? Are you relaxed with who you are? And are you a positive influence on your mate?

There are those moments in every relationship where we may feel the need to hide certain aspects of our identity so that we don't offend or upset our mate, and sometimes we have scars that we just don't want anyone to see. But be careful that your embarrassment, shame, or fear doesn't become a pattern or excuse for excluding your spouse from these parts of your life. I counsel so many couples who hold on to these secrets and ultimately find themselves in unhealthy relationships outside their marriage. They open up and share who they really are with another person who is not their spouse, which can lead to trouble. God gives us relationships of destiny to become comfortable sharing who we are without it costing us anything. We should be able to share the most intimate details of who we are with our mate and it be OK. But this kind of sharing demands trust and a pattern of love and acceptance from the other person. It may take a while, because some wounds are very deep and may still feel fresh. Some scars are ugly. So be patient and kind.

One of the other things I've learned is that when I allow Stephaine to be who she is in our marriage, it creates room for me to be who I am. Things that I like should not be forfeited or discarded simply because we are married. Neither should the things she enjoys. I enjoy shopping, playing basketball, traveling, and a host of other things. If my relationship with Stephaine caused me to give up the things that I enjoy, life wouldn't be fun anymore. That's why when you allow God to bring you together with the right person with the right personality, that person is prepared to embrace the healthy things that you enjoy without forcing you to choose between what you enjoy and the relationship.

## *Our Uniqueness Serves God's Purpose*

One of the things I've learned over the years about ministry is that God uses our personalities within the context of our call. We all have a call from God to be His witnesses and help bring in His kingdom, whether we are teachers, bankers, plumbers, retail clerks—whatever. As you know by now, my call is to be a pastor, and God uses who I am as a person in my ministry. My personality comes through in the way I hold meetings, the way I pray at someone's bedside, and the way I preach where my members often pick up on my humor, passions, and concerns. Your personality comes through too. It comes through with things like how you deal with people, how you present yourself, and how effective you are. It is your uniqueness that allows God to be present and work His purpose through you. We each have special gifts and abilities that God can use to bring about His kingdom. And there are people only you can witness to. I, as a pastor, or Stephaine, as a doctor, may not be able to reach them. But being a couple of destiny means that what you are on the inside, with your gift and abilities, is reflected in how you appear as a couple to the world.

### *You Enhance My Identity*

I have seen so many people who were miserable internally even though their relationship looked great externally. Their mates were doing great things, but something was amiss. The visions and dreams of the support person were being suppressed and dying slowly. Can you imagine the level of pain associated with unrealized dreams? Just as it is important not to give up who you are as a person, it is not God's will for you to sacrifice your dreams on the altar of a relationship. Relationships of destiny don't permit that. I've witnessed young people put their education on hold to support their mates and never go back to college. Support has its place, but it should never result in the demise of your own vision. Your identity should be affirmed and embraced. Your relationship should enhance you and not diminish you. If only one person's needs are met and the other person's are minimized, this sows seeds of discord and bitterness that will eventually bloom into discontent.

Stephaine is full of vision. Although she supports what God does through my life one hundred percent, I recognize that He is using her to touch the world as well. Every chance I get, I affirm her and encourage her to manifest her vision. When her vision is successful, our home is successful. I want her to know that I am not diminished by the greatness in her; I am enhanced. When we are in public settings, I enjoy when people recognize her gifts and contributions rather than refer to her as a supportive wife to me. She is that, but she is so much more.

The amazing thing about maintaining our identity within the relationship is what God does as a result of it. The more Stephaine and I grow in our marriage, the more we discover how similar we are. Although we affirm each others' uniqueness, we also recognize that God intertwines our visions. When Stephaine founded her nonprofit organization, Full Circle Healthy Community Coalition, she had a purpose. That purpose is to be a connector of resources to the folks in the community. There were a lot of great resources available to assist people, but nobody knew what or where they were. Stephaine was able to develop a resource locator that connects people to resources and resources to people. It is a brilliant idea and quite effective in helping people in the community. As I continued to cast vision within the church, God gave me the theme "Healing the House." Our ministry focus was on healthy lifestyle and awareness. Although Stephaine and I both heard from God about two independent visions, they have converged to bless our church and the community. That's how God works. He always has a plan, and all we have to do is follow it.

God always has a plan. All we have to do is follow it.

How is God working in your life to intertwine your visions? Do you share each other's goals and dreams? What is your vision for a successful home, work environment, marriage? What are the characteristics of a marriage that is solid and does not just look solid? While we don't want others to define us, we still witness to the world, so how others see us is important. How does your marriage appear to other people? Do they think it is on a path of destiny?

****

## Stephaine's Story

As you know, Joseph is a pastor and, being married to a pastor, when I meet people for the first time they will often ask me, "So how long have you been in the ministry?" I always find this question a bit awkward to answer because what they usually assume is that my primary career revolves around Joseph and the church; and it does not. Although I do not minister from the pulpit, I know that I *do* minister through working as a doctor in the hospital, by mentoring graduate students, and by just being me. My life (as well as yours) is a "walking" ministry each and every day.

Joseph made it very clear to me from day one that he wanted me to continue to simply be me; he had no other expectations than that. He went out of his way to explain to his staff and the congregation before we got married that I was coming to Nashville to be HIS wife. He let everyone know I had my own separate career and interests that I would continue to pursue. PERIOD. It was very important that I heard that from him. It tremendously eased my anxiety as I made my transition to being his wife. He understood better than I the pressures that could be placed on me from the church and others in the faith-based community to conform to a certain model or expectation of what a pastors' wife or First Lady is expected to do, to be, to look like, or to dress like. As Joseph said earlier, within the church community, people often refer to the pastor's wife as First Lady, and this title carries with it respect, admiration, *and* expectations. And it did take me a while to accept the title. But Joseph never made me feel like I had to fit a certain mold or act a certain way. He's made it so easy for me to just be myself. I do those things I enjoy doing. I am not pressured to do things I do not enjoy doing or don't feel called to do. I have my own sense of style. One of the first things that pops into people's minds when they think of women in the church is wearing large hats. No, I don't wear big hats to church, or at all for that matter. Not that there aren't countless amazingly beautiful hats, but I'm just not a hat person. It's not for me. Mind you, there are a lot of women who do and do it well. To each her own!

### *Being Who You Choose to Be*

It's critical when you are moving into any new setting that you know who you are first and foremost. People have their expectations of who you should be, how you should act, what that should look like. But you can't own that. You cannot control other people's expectations. All you can control is who you choose to be and how you choose to act or react. By nature, I am a people person and love talking and interacting with others. But if I didn't know who I was or have a strong sense of self already, I would run the risk of yielding to everyone else's expectations of who I am supposed to be, which would be disastrous.

One thing I have come to realize is that, yes, everyone has an opinion and is genuinely entitled to it, but at the end of the day only three opinions really count for me and how I am going to live my life: God's, mine, and my husband's. As long as these three are pleased, I'm right where I need to be, doing exactly what I need to be doing.

### *Walking in Purpose*

Several months into our marriage, I found myself feeling empty. Now mind you, I was a newlywed, married to this amazing man, living in a new city, in a beautiful home, with everything I could ever think to want within my reach. Joseph and I were busy, but by this time I had a better handle on things. We were traveling quite a bit, and when we weren't traveling together I was working in the hospital. Of course, we also attended a number of church functions where I was getting to know more and more of the congregants and them me. Looking from the outside in, I'm certain the average person would think, wow, she's got it all. Ironically, though, I began to feel a huge void that I couldn't shake. I wasn't happy, and I couldn't understand why. As Joseph said earlier, things looked good on the outside but were unsettled on the inside.

I found myself praying daily for an answer so that I could fix it! What exactly would I fix? I wasn't sure. But it was clear that something wasn't right. One morning when I was journaling, the Holy Spirit spoke to me and helped me realize that despite all of the material things around me, I wasn't really living. Don't get me wrong. Our life was wonderful. I absolutely loved my husband without a doubt in my mind. I loved being married. I was tremendously thankful for all that we had been blessed with over the past year and a half, including our newly expanding circle of family and friends. Despite all of this, though, I realized that a part of me was dying. Our schedules were full. We were very busy, which was great, but I did not feel like I was walking in my purpose, which is why my soul felt so empty. This was the void I had been struggling to identify.

Anyone who knows me understands two things about me. One, I firmly believe that EVERYTHING happens for a reason, even though on occasion we ourselves can't always understand why. Early in our courting, when Joseph and I realized what was transpiring between us, we talked about the fact that God had brought us together not simply for ourselves but for a much greater purpose, likely far greater than anything we could ever comprehend at the moment. We could look at each other and see that God was clearly in the business of blessing us beyond anything we could dream of for ourselves. I knew that God moved me from Boston to Nashville to do something different. I did not know what exactly, but I was certain that if God wanted me to do the same thing I was doing in Boston, He would have left me there.

> Everything happens for a reason.

The second thing that people around me know is that I wholeheartedly believe that a life without meaning and direction is not really a life at all. Everyone has a purpose and every life has a meaning, but we each must be open to exploring and discovering what that is for ourselves. For me, if I feel like I am not walking in my purpose and using my skills or gifts to benefit others, I am not fulfilled. That's where I found myself—busy yet unfulfilled, as opposed to being productive, walking in my purpose and full of life. I realized that, as a result, my spirit was unsettled. I had to come to terms with the fact that over the last few months, with the hustle and bustle of everything, I had begun to lose my focus, my self, and my involvement with some of the core activities that drive me.

I had to be honest with myself and confess that much of what I was doing was a result of me trying to keep pace with Joseph as opposed to doing what I felt led by God to do. Funny thing is, I decided before we got married that I would "just be me" and do what I wanted to do—nothing more, nothing less. The issue is it was easier said than done. When you get married to your best friend, you want to spend time together doing those things that are important to you both. However, in our case, with our increasingly hectic schedule, we found ourselves going, going, going and doing, doing, doing—but most of it had to do with Joseph and his schedule, meetings, and speaking engagements.

Don't get me wrong. No one put a gun to my head. I was actually a willing participant. I absolutely enjoy being present and supporting my husband in his endeavors. I think that's why it took a little while for me to understand what had me feeling so empty. I was present for him yet absent for myself, and no matter how you try to sugarcoat it, that can never be healthy—not for yourself, your spouse, or your marriage. I remember that initially it would manifest as my becoming short with Joseph in our conversations; then that slowly turned into open frustration but with no cause or warrant, or so I thought. I honestly had no idea where it was coming from. It worried me quite a bit, and I know he didn't understand it either.

Over the next few weeks I found myself seeking God more and more, reaffirming why He wanted me here in Nashville, what my purpose was and what direction He wanted me to take. Over and over God would talk to me about educating and empowering, mentoring, and serving—themes that He had held fairly constant in my life up to this point. Only this time He began to reveal more to me in terms of new adventures that would challenge me and take me FAR outside of my comfort zone. I was nervous and excited at the same time. I could feel myself starting to realign with HIM. I was full of life again! I knew I didn't have all of the answers. However, I did know that my purpose was much greater then just being married to a pastor and working at the hospital (although I obviously loved both). I realized God expected more from me—much more than ever before. Talk about pressure! But I was honestly OK with it all.

> You must take time to pour not only into your mate but into yourself.

This period of time really helped me understand what people meant when they would say that in marriage you must take time to pour not only into your mate but into yourself as well on a regular basis. You have to take time to steal away for yourself, even if means just going to dinner with a friend or burrowing into a good book. This helps you to not lose yourself in the midst of the everyday chaos, and, most important, it provides a time when you can reconnect with yourself and with God so that you can stay in line with what God's desire is for your life.

Now, things are awesome! Not perfect, but perfect for Joseph and me. I have learned to just do what I do best, which is to simply be me, stay "in my lane" and walk unapologetically in my God-given purpose. This doesn't mean that I only do those things that are easy or familiar. Rather, for me, this refers to the fact that I really try to do only those things that I feel called to do—things that align with God's vision for my life. I've come to realize that it really is just that simple. Yes, I support my husband, but no I don't have to go to EVERY event and gathering at the church or go to ALL of Joseph's speaking engagements. I love him and support him unconditionally, and he knows it. So I don't have to go to every engagement or travel with him every single time he goes out of town. For one thing, it's not feasible based on our respective schedules, but it's also not healthy for any marriage to focus so much on the other person that you begin to lose the essence of who you are. It's also not conducive to all of the other wonderful things God wants to birth through you.

Joseph and I are no less busy than we were before, but now I know without a shadow of a doubt that those things I am spending my time doing are all things I feel called to do. Following God's will has led me to start a local community-based nonprofit organization called Full Circle Healthy Community Coalition, which serves to actively connect people in the community to the local health-related resources and services available to them in order to help families achieve optimal health. Joseph and I have a foundation dedicated to increasing opportunities for higher education and empowering young people. I still work as a physician in the intensive care unit for infants. There I take care of premature and sick infants and also teach medical students and other young doctors in training. I am also involved in the healthy living, healthy lifestyle initiatives and other related activities at the church, as well as a number of other endeavors in organizations all over the city.

When I'm not working in the hospital, Joseph and I can still be found traveling up to two or three times a week for various engagements. Only now, because I regularly take time out (even if for just a few minutes a day) to reconnect and realign with God, the dynamics of our life are infinitely different and more conducive to a healthier, happier marriage. I am me. Yes, I am still known by many as Bishop Walker's wife; I can't run from that and frankly do not want to—I absolutely love my husband. But at the same time, many others know me as Dr. Walker or Dr. Stephaine or simply Stephaine, and they also know that I am a multidimensional, complex being who loves the Lord and loves serving others in whatever capacity I feel led. Despite my husband and I being extremely busy, I am loving life! I feel like I am certainly flowing in my gifts and using what God has blessed us with to be a blessing for others. After all, for me that's what makes life worth living.

****

## KEEPING UP YOUR ANTENNA

EVERY ACTION HAS A REACTION. If we find ourselves reacting to our mates in ways that puzzle them, perhaps we don't know them as well as we should. Perhaps the issue is our assumptions rather than their behavior. Perhaps our assumptions are birthed out of a lack of knowledge about who they are. So the more we understand each other's identities, the more we can know each other's heart; and because we know each other's heart, we can recognize each other's strengths and weaknesses. And we can trust our mates to tell us the truth about our own strengths and weaknesses.

When you get down to the basics of this issue, it really is a spiritual matter. The late Dr. Samuel Dewitt Proctor once said, "Always keep your spiritual antenna up." This is something Stephaine and I carry daily. We want to always be sensitive to what God is doing in the spirit. Relationships of destiny are not carnal. They are spiritual. If you are not a spiritual person, you quickly lose sight of why God has brought you together. You will never appreciate the uniqueness that God has placed within your mate nor be able to understand your mate's changes properly. What we have attempted to do in marriage is keep up our antennas. We recognize that revelation comes from God, and it is God who ultimately makes all things known. We recognize that and rely heavily on God to reveal to us each other's ever-changing identity. This is important for the survival of our relationship. We make a demand upon ourselves to never lose sight of this.

Is your antenna up? Are you taking adequate time to understand the identity of your mate? Are you so consumed elsewhere that you feel you have lost sight of who you are in your relationship? It's never too late to reconnect. God is speaking to you now as you read this book to slow down and go back to those things that really matter. Once you step away from the hustle and bustle, schedules, appointments, and deadlines, you will discover so many wonderful things about yourself as well as your mate. Your relationship of destiny won't rob you of who you are; it will embrace and enhance you both.

## Talking Points

1. What are three or four words you would use to describe your mate?

2. How has your relationship changed since you first started dating or first married? Is your relationship maturing in a healthy direction? Do you fight more or less? Do you fight over the same things you did early on?

3. How have you matured since you first started dating or first married? Are you more or less patient? More or less trusting? More or less spiritual? More or less at peace with each other?

4. In what ways do you show consideration to the wishes of your spouse?

5. Are there areas in your life that you don't want to change? How do these match up with what your spouse wants you to be?

6. Name your mate's favorite color, leisure activity, Scripture passage, and food.

7. Who or what comes first in your home? God? Self? Marriage? Children? Job? Spouse? TV? Other?

8. Write a vision statement for your marriage.

## Chapter 6

# FINDING BALANCE

MANY COUPLES ARE SIMPLY OVERWHELMED by day-to-day living. What is your life like? Are you juggling responsibilities, expectations, conflicts? When something is always up in the air, when you find yourself juggling all the time, it is difficult to find balance and peace of mind. As the pastor of a twenty-five-thousand-member congregation, alongside a wife who is a neonatologist, as a couple we have some interesting opportunities to find balance. Every decision that we make affects us both. Sometimes we feel like we work in air traffic control. Managing our lives is complicated. The engagements, meetings, functions, and family obligations are just a few of the things that make up our lives. What we knew going in was that we would have to be strategic and intentional about maintaining balance. But we believe that it is God's will that our lives are in proper balance. Paul tells the church at Corinth that everything must "be done decently and in order" (1 Corinthians 14:40).

### EITHER YOU LIVE LIFE OR IT WILL LIVE YOU

WE REALIZE THAT THIS IS A VERY sensitive area for many folks. There never seems to be enough time in the day to keep things going the way they need to go. Countless couples we know are overwhelmed because their lives are out of balance; they don't recognize the importance of priorities or the cost of not making them. Jesus spoke a powerful word in Matthew 6:33. It is a word about balance and priorities: "Seek ye first the kingdom of God, and his righteousness; and all these things shall be added unto you." When I refer to *kingdom,* I am referring to God's way of doing things. His ways keep us balanced. Whenever other things take priority over the kingdom of God, life gets out of balance. We run after things and run ourselves down. We end up frustrated, and it manifests in our relationship. We are short with each other and often irritated by the slightest things. It's all because we have failed to establish priorities.

When two people come together there are numerous things going on all the time in their respective lives, so making priorities is a must. One of the things that we had to do as a couple was establish priorities by setting aside days that would be just *our* days. We call them our Sabbath days. No matter what is going on, we will not allow the hustle and bustle of our professions to cross that boundary. We need the time just to be together and pour into each other. When there is no balance, both persons end up empty. God pours into us, and we pour out to thousands of cups of those who wait to be filled each week, whether at church or at the hospital. For a time, we both came home with an expectation to be filled again, because we were both empty. This is when we recognized the need to step back and evaluate our schedules and take control of them. Either you live life or it will live you.

Do you have times that you set aside just for being together? How do you make your marriage a priority? What part does God play in your priorities? Would your relationship benefit from finding Sabbath time? Try making a list of the ten things you want to do together in the next year and make a promise to each other to begin this week.

It is essential to your relationship that you carve out time for you and your mate. The work will always be there, but your spouse won't. The work will not stop. The demands won't stop coming. There will always be another meeting or event you could attend. You've got to live in the midst of all of it and realize that healthy relationships are ones where work stops or at least is put on hold. Start today by blocking out dates for you and your mate. Put "fences" around them. Protect them. This is your time. This is the time that you and your mate can be refreshed by being together.

## Joseph's Story

FROM THE BEGINNING WE WERE clear that our marriage was our priority. Although I am a pastor and minister to people around the world, my first ministry is my marriage. After God, my life has to revolve around my marriage. I've seen so many Christian leaders lose balance and take on more than they should, at the risk of putting their family time on the back burner. When my home is happy, I'm happy. It is important that I make my investments there so that I am able to be more effective in my ministry.

### *Learning to Say No*

It is important that my staff and church understand what my first priority is so that there will be no misunderstanding. I've had to learn to say no. Prior to getting married, I was incredibly busy. I am still quite busy these days, but my life is better managed around priorities. I could not take my life as it existed prior to marriage and continue to work without regard to how it would influence my relationship. If your relationship of destiny is important to you, it should be a priority. You should never sacrifice your family on the altar of work.

### *Put Your Life in Proper Order*

There is a powerful teaching in Exodus about balance. We all know what happened when Moses was taking on too much and was told to share the load, but the initial revelation happens when God first calls him. God calls Moses out of a bush that's on fire but the fire does not consume it. While God could have just called Moses and given him his assignment, the question that must be asked is why would God need the theatrics of a burning bush? Was there something God was saying through this miraculous event? Yes, there was. God wanted to give Moses a burning for his mission.

*When God gives an assignment, have a burning for it, but never let it burn you out.* The moment it burns you out is the moment you've stepped outside of His will and are out of balance. The reason so many of us are overwhelmed and worn out is because we are taking on more than God intends. It doesn't matter what theological language you attach to it, when you are out of balance your relationships will never be effective.

One of the things Stephaine helped me with was organizing priorities. I didn't know how to say no. I have now learned that sometimes no is an appropriate answer. I have so many things competing for my time, but it is important to *first* put things in their proper order. Take a look at your life and prioritize. Don't allow weeks to go by and get so busy that things get out of balance. Take control of your life. Sometimes that means pausing and evaluating things as they are and working together to put in place a new system that works for you.

### *Time for Just Us*

Once you've set priorities in your relationship, it is important to set boundaries. Boundaries act like fences; they protect and keep unwanted distractions out of your life. Boundaries show other people what you value. But boundaries can be difficult because we sometimes feel obligated to give others access to our personal lives. That is the nature of ministry and medicine, but it is also the nature of living in today's world for many of us. When I first meet Stephaine, I discovered that we were both very relational. We love people and enjoy socializing. For us, this meant that we regularly had folks over to our home. We enjoy hanging out with friends. Though this is important to both of us, we had to set boundaries for ourselves. It wasn't that people were forcing their way into our personal space. We have some amazing friends and we truly enjoy spending time with them. The issue with us is realizing that we need some "us" time. We had to establish boundaries and learn the balance between spending time with others and enjoying ourselves alone.

"Us" time is important for any relationship to survive. The socializing bug consistently hit us, and we found ourselves planning things and wondering who could go with us. After much contemplation, it hit us. We need to take some trips alone. We need to have some parties by ourselves. We need to play cards and games together. If you find your relationship being crowded out by other people, you must ask yourself if you've established proper boundaries. Friends are important, but couples should do things together by themselves while encouraging each other and doing fun family things. Appropriate boundaries will help you find balance between time with friends and time for "us."

Boundaries can be difficult to establish, especially when there are many demands on your time. And there are times when your boundaries have to have some built-in flexibility, especially when children, friends, and family are involved. Rigid boundaries can become unhealthy barriers if we are not wise. But people do need to know that your relationship is a priority. One way to show them is to ask them how they maintain their own boundaries.

### *A Manageable Lifestyle*

We've discussed priorities and boundaries, but let's also discuss balance in more detail. When we think of balance we should think of a manageable lifestyle. There are some things in our lives that are inevitable, things that we have to deal with whether we want to or not. For some, it's late hours on the job; for others, it's the children and all the obligations that come as a result. Some people are required to travel a lot, while others are required to meet aggressive deadlines. Regardless of these realities, it is important that you develop a system to manage it all. One thing we found is that, by pursuing destiny, your schedule may not get easier. Stephaine and I came to the conclusion that this is our reality and we needed to find ways to manage our schedule so it would reflect our priorities and values.

One of the things that we often overlook is the itinerary of Jesus. Jesus had much on His schedule that would change as quickly as it had been set. For example, Jairus asked Jesus to come to his house because his daughter was dying. On the way there, a woman hemorrhaging blood interrupted His schedule. The amazing thing about Jesus' schedule was how He responded to it. He was in control of it and managed it with balance. He never allowed others to dictate His time frame. Another example: when Lazarus was sick, the family requested that He come right away. Jesus purposely took His time because He knew what would happen when He got there. What a great lesson for us to learn. Don't allow other people to dictate how you manage your life. Stay on your schedule, and you will be effective.

I had to learn this lesson early in my ministry. I would always respond to everyone's crises immediately, often at the same time. I almost burned myself out, until I realized that I could only do what I was physically able to do, and I had to inform others that I would get around to them as soon as I was able. This has carried over into my relationships. People still make demands upon my life, but I have learned to manage those demands better. For instance, Stephaine and I make our holiday plans at the beginning of each year. This is important because sharing holidays with family is something we value and believe in. The challenge of my profession is that folks sometimes want to get married during certain holidays and request my presence. There was a time I would rearrange my personal plans to accommodate their wedding plans. Now, wisdom prevails. For my life to balance, I have to make sure I don't spend my holidays working and have my family miss out. I even made it a policy in our church that no weddings take place during the holidays, because I realized the position it put many of my staff members in as well. People don't often think about the impact of something like this when they are making plans. It's not something that usually comes up on their radar. But because my marriage is my priority and we've set boundaries, I have to make sure that I balance my family's needs with the needs of others, and I have to make sure that the family needs of my staff are also respected.

Most of you reading this book can probably think of times when you've allowed your relationship to get out of balance. All of us can think of times when we've allowed other things to take priority over the needs of our relationship—and then everything goes flying. This is why God is giving you this word now. You must understand the importance of balance. You cannot be lopsided and expect your relationship to work well.

### *Follow Your Assignments*

Before Stephaine and I married, I had lived my life so out of balance that I felt guilty having time away from ministry. The needs were so great that I felt it was important to be there for people *all* the time. God spoke to me about this some years ago. The word He gave me was that Jesus never followed needs. He followed His assignments. There will always be needs.

Many of us feel that it's our responsibility to do it all. I've seen so many marriages fail and children grow bitter because one person in the family is out of balance. The fact that Jesus didn't follow needs is clearly seen in the story of Lazarus. There were a lot of people who were dead the day Lazarus died, but they were not Jesus' assignment. When He went to the tombs, He called Lazarus by name. He had to be specific, because He had so much power. If He had simply said, "Get up," everybody would have gotten up. He called Lazarus by his name. That day, Lazarus was the assignment even though others were dead too. I've learned to focus on my assignment. I have so many engagement requests that I could speak every day of the week, fifty-two weeks a year. I have to pray about what my assignment is. I have to make sure that I'm not pouring out around the world and not pouring out at home. I have to make sure that I'm not just blessing everybody else's house and not blessing my own.

### *Work Hard; Play Harder*

Stephaine and I have these incredible moments of refuge where we steal away from the chaos and reconnect with each other. One threat to every relationship is becoming so busy that you neglect the things that are most important. A part of managing life and having balance is the rule: "Work hard; play harder." Stephaine reintroduced this principle to me. Recognizing that we both carry enormous responsibilities, we know we have to do fun stuff. We know that if we don't, we will be consumed and never truly have a life—or a life together. So when we go somewhere, we lay down our work and simply enjoy life spontaneously. We enjoy amusement parks, shopping, going to concerts. These and a host of other things bring balance to our relationship. I used to be concerned about what other people thought about seeing me out having fun, but I have to do what is important for me, for Stephaine, and for us.

### *Proper Alignment*

Having Sabbath times and fun times is also about ordering your life. When Paul speaks about things being done in decency and order, he speaks to us all. The word that sticks out in this text is "order." Order means that things are in proper alignment. Paul speaks in 1 Corinthians 12 about the gifts of the church in association with the body of Christ. This comparison to the body is important because it speaks to each member functioning properly in its place and in relationship to the others. Think about it for a moment. The right arm cannot say to the left, "I don't need you." Both arms need each other. More important, they need each other to be in proper alignment to the other parts for the body to function effectively. The same is true in your relationship as a couple. All the components that make up your lives together are complex. And each one needs to be in proper alignment or balance so that your relationship can function in order. If one person is overwhelmed at work by taking on more than what's necessary, it will throw the relationship out of kilter and cause tension at home. If one person is overwhelmed at home, it will also throw the relationship out of kilter and cause tension at work. All the components of our lives need to work in harmony if a relationship of destiny is going to blossom.

Balance is not easy. It is a daily challenge for us. To be sure, there will be things that come up that you can't control; but if you have a system in place to manage it, it will have less impact on your relationship. Stephaine and I are aware that either one of our phones might ring at three in the morning. Someone might be in a critical situation and need us. We have developed the kind of balance that, when that happens, we support each other. Although these times are few and far between, because we do so many other amazing things together, these sacrifices are easier to make. And while they may bring stress, they won't break our marriage. It's all about having things in order, being in control of your schedule, and demanding balance.

### *Process, Process, Process*

As you strive to achieve balance in your life, remember this: just like every other area we've discussed in this book, it is a process. In fact, you might even go through withdrawal when you begin setting priorities and boundaries. You may be so used to chaos that balance seems odd. For example, I remember dropping everything and taking time away only to struggle with trying to find a way to check on things at work—even on my honeymoon. As a pastor, I have to learn to find balance, and it remains a continuing process. I remember telling a friend that I had not taken a "real" vacation in years. The demands of my ministry and the response of my congregation when I was absent forced me into an unhealthy practice of being present all the time, at the expense of taking time off for myself. Every advisor, scholar, and counselor tells me how unwise this is, but my argument was the same. If I am not there, the people won't come; and consequently it will set us back and create more headaches when I return.

You may be the same way, but I've also heard many pastors say the same thing. A dear friend who pastors a relatively large church once shared with me that he had had a heart attack a few months prior because he would not slow down. The words that he shared with me were so powerful, they changed my life. He said while he was in the hospital, the Lord came to him and said, "Give me back my church." What a revelation. I was holding on to something that never belonged to me. It's God's church, and He will always take care of it. Do you feel guilty leaving the job or family to take some time away as a couple? It's God's world. He can take care of it and you.

****

## STEPHAINE'S STORY

PRIOR TO GETTING MARRIED, Joseph and I understood and talked about how, as individuals in our respective lives, we were continuously pulled in various directions, whether it be by family or work or the ministry. We recognized from the beginning that we would have to work hard at maintaining a healthy sense of "us," both as a couple and as individuals in the midst of it all. We could not possibly allow ourselves to work so hard or pour out to others so much that we had nothing to give when it came to pouring into each other.

As Joseph mentioned above, play is important—especially when you work hard. My life philosophy has always been "Work hard and play harder." In my profession as an intensive care doctor, this was how I normally found balance and stayed sane. When I'm on, I'm on. But when I'm off, boy, am I off. However, when we first married, it seemed like Joseph's life philosophy was, "Work, work, work some more, maybe take a brief break for a day or so, then hurry up and get back to work." Needless to say, I knew before getting married that I was certainly in for a challenge. I also knew that this was one reason God in His infinite wisdom put Joseph and me together, so that we could help each other find a healthy sustainable sense of balance in our individual lives as well as our marriage.

I had to come to terms with that fact that, because Joseph was a pastor who preached every Sunday, our weekends were no longer our own. Joseph was used to this, as this was simply a way of life for him. But for me, it took a minute to wrap my mind around the fact that our weekends were now our busiest workdays. So not only are we "on" during the week but we are also "on" over the weekend. When would we possibly get a break? In no way was this conducive to a healthy marriage or a healthy life. But what were we going to do? There are only so many hours in the day. We would have to figure out what would work for us in the context of our new life together. Gone were days of one-to-two-week vacations and simple weekend getaways—or so I thought.

### *The Luxury of Being Away*

One thing about Joseph is that, in this day and age of technological advances, he found it difficult to truly "be away" even when he was able to get away. I remember our honeymoon. We got married on a Saturday and flew out on the first flight Sunday morning. It was the first time in almost five years that Joseph had not been present at church and had not preached on a Sunday. He seemed so anxious, fidgeting in his seat the entire flight. He was constantly checking his phone and computer for communication from the church. We were gone for two entire weeks, and although we were enjoying ourselves, at moments it seemed almost torturous for him. Joseph was used to going on mini-getaways for a day or two here or there. Never had he taken a break to this extent. By the time the second Sunday rolled around, I will never forget, I awoke at 3 a.m. Here we are, in the middle of the Mediterranean Sea, surrounded by beautiful island paradise, and what do I see? Joseph logging onto the computer to watch Mt. Zion's Sunday service through the online streaming faith webcast. It was like watching an addict. He just could not let go even for a little while. In that moment, I honestly felt bad for him. He had been working so constantly for so many years that he didn't really know how to let go and take time for himself. It was as if he felt guilty doing so—as if the entire church would implode if he were not there. I eventually realized that just like it took me time to adjust to my new reality, it was going to take him time to adjust to learning to find balance in his, now our, life as well.

### *Schedule Time for Each Other*

Once we returned to the states, our schedules were so hectic that we very quickly recognized that if we did not physically schedule time together on our actual work calendars, the chances of it happening were slim to none. Also, if his staff did not see anything scheduled in a time slot, although *to us* it was a day off, we would find them calling, asking him to get involved in something, or even worse, we would look up and they would have scheduled him for an important meeting. So we literally were forced to put our scheduled time together into our respective calendars. So yes, although it may sound funny or even a bit over the top to some, we sit down together and schedule our time together like we schedule meetings. At times we may look at the calendar months in advance. Doing so allows us to plan ahead with no excuses, and if we can block out an entire day or two, we do it. We realize that if we are not deliberate about defining time for "just us" then every day magically gets filled with meetings and events. We eventually come up for air only to ask, "What happened to the time?" The reality is that no one knows our personal schedule or the expectations we set in our marriage except for us, so it's no one's responsibility except ours to make time for the most important gift that God has blessed us with—each other.

How do you manage your calendars? Do you keep a family calendar? Is it updated? Do you both have easy access to it?

Early on in our marriage, given that Sundays are Joseph's most strenuous workdays, he would often take the following day, Monday, to recoup and relax. My schedule at the hospital is flexible enough to allow me to have a couple of open days a week. As a result, we chose Mondays as our rest and reunite days. We decided that we could do anything we wanted EXCEPT for schedule meetings or appointments with other people. Some days we would spend the entire day together. Other days we might take a portion of the day for ourselves separately and spend the remainder together. We might go shopping, run errands together, go to the park, ride bikes, play tennis, or simply "veg out" and do nothing but lie on the couch and watch movies. It totally depended on what our respective needs were at the time. Although we had etched this day in stone as "our day," we left it flexible enough to meet us wherever we were for the moment, so that if we needed time for ourselves we could take it and not feel guilty. Ultimately our goal for the day was that, regardless of what we did, we ended the day feeling refreshed and restored.

What do you like to do on your days off? Do you ever get to "veg out"? Is this something you enjoy?

### *Restore, Reconnect, Revive*

As time went on, we began to realize that although taking a day during the week to reconnect was a good start for us, given that Joseph was not one to regularly rest and take a break for himself, we needed more. Because we knew our Mondays were essentially free days for us, we found ourselves beginning to save things to do for that day. So much so, that eventually those Mondays turned into "let's run errands all day together days" or "let's catch up on work from home days." On occasion this was great because we felt productive, but usually it meant that by the end of the day, since we were trying to squeeze in so much, we were exhausted—which completely defeated the purpose. We realized that we needed to figure out how to get out of Nashville, not to work or travel to an engagement but simply to rest, relax, and get away from it all without the phones and computers to distract us. Although this wasn't something Joseph was used to doing on a regular basis, he could see the toll that not doing so was taking on both of us.

Although taking spontaneous weekend getaways to reconnect as a couple was not an option, we learned to take full advantage of the infrequent gaps in our calendars during the week. We started off by identifying quick twenty-four-hour gaps in our schedule to just get away for the day. Then eventually, one day turned into two days, and now on occasion sometimes we find ourselves being able to get away for three. As you can see, we may not have gotten it right the first time, but because we were committed to prioritizing our marriage and finding time to pour back into each other, we've managed to eventually find a system that works.

It's taken Joseph some time to get to a place of comfort in taking time for himself, but now he sees it as a necessary component of maintaining balance in our marriage. He poured out so much to everyone else that even others around us began telling him he needed to take a break and take time out for himself. As his wife, I accepted it as my ministry to help my husband learn to seek that place of balance. I recognized the toll a hectic schedule like ours can take on the body and the mind. I love Joseph and want him to be around for a long time. Now he sees that, although the church needs a pastor, they love him and me enough to let him recuperate and rest in order to make sure that he remains healthy and is still around years from now. Nowadays, it's not unusual to find him carving out two to three days at a time for us to get away to reconnect. Although these trips don't come frequently, when they do happen, they are usually right on time. They basically equate to a weekend getaway, only now they're in the middle of the week, which is just wonderful!

Another lesson we've learned is to take full advantage of work-related travel. When Joseph travels to other cities to minister, I try to travel with him as much as I can. On occasion, when our schedule permits, we may decide to go a day or so earlier or stay a day or so later, essentially converting a part of the trip into a mini-vacation. Sometimes we make plans. Sometime we don't. Even if we don't make plans to do anything on those extra days, just being able to not have to rush to and from the airport and having an opportunity to relax or sleep in is much appreciated.

It's not uncommon for us to stay somewhere an extra night only to wake up at ten or eleven o'clock the next morning, which for my early-rising husband is a big deal. But I always say that it's simply our bodies telling us that we need to slow down, and we must learn to listen to that. The fact that we often have no clue how exhausted we are until we get still and sit down can be frightening to comprehend.

You simply set aside uninterrupted time to spend together and actually do just that.

While you may not be able to take trips, there are other ways to get away from it all—turning off cell phones is a good start or listening to some music as you sit together on the deck. The important thing is not where you go or what you do but the fact that you simply set aside uninterrupted time to spend together and actually do just that.

Family is tremendously important to both Joseph and me. We both come from very large families, so as you can imagine there are constantly events or occasions that we would love to attend but may not be able to. Early on in our marriage, as we were trying to find free time for "just us," attending family events was relegated mainly to the holidays. Once we found a cadence within our marriage and began to feel like we had finally found a place of balance (however fluid), we felt we were then able to integrate the rest of our family. His family is mainly in Shreveport and my family is split between Los Angeles and D.C. Although we sought to see our families together as much as we could, these occasions weren't as frequent as we had hoped. As it turned out, this was because we continued to be quite protective of our time for just the two of us. If we had time to go see others, then it also meant that we could use that time to spend together alone, so we would simply opt to do just that. So instead, what we've found has worked most recently is being able to visit our respective families even if it means going alone.

When I find that my schedule at work is exceptionally strenuous, if Joseph chooses he will go see his family or friends during that time. Although it makes sense that I do the same when his work is unusually strenuous, ironically, I often feel torn. Due to the pace of our lives, when I have an opportunity to travel to go see my family, Joseph often has obligations with the church. I often feel like I too should be present at whatever the activity or event is. Joseph, however, will often put his foot down and virtually force me to go—and I always return rejuvenated, thanking him for knowing me so well. He's my husband. He knows it's important to me to spend time with those close to me, but he also sees the struggle I am having as I feel a responsibility to the church to be present as much as I can.

People at Mt. Zion are awesome, and I genuinely enjoy spending time at church-related activities and functions. Joseph does an amazing job helping me give myself the release to not feel guilty when I leave to spend much-needed time away with my family or friends. If we waited until we both could travel, that might encroach on our "us" time. In addition, it would mean fewer opportunities to connect with the family and friends we love and hold dear. So we do what we can when we can, and it works out for us.

As you can see, we've learned to balance our life in a way that is conducive to both our careers and our personalities. I can't say it's always easy. It's certainly a work in progress. At times we feel as if we've found that perfect balance. Then there are other instances when we stand around wondering where all the time has gone and how we can fit everything in. We try to be creative and think outside of the box. But ultimately it's through open and honest communication, listening, deliberate planning, and a bit of old-fashioned trial and error that we are able to figure out solutions that are healthy not only for us as individuals but also for our marriage.

****

## BALANCE LEADS TO ABUNDANT LIVING

MANY OF YOU READING THIS book struggle to let go of certain things because you carry their burden all the time. The real question to consider is this: What will happen if you die? This sounds harsh, but you must consider it. Jesus came that we might have life and life more abundantly. It is essential that we recognize the importance of ministering to ourselves so that we can minister to our mates. Abundance is the product of proper connection. When Jesus said in John 15 that He is the true vine and that the branches bear fruit through the connection with Him, He gave us a powerful revelation. Jesus said that His Father takes care of the garden. This suggests that when branches need attention, the Father makes sure they are taken care of. If branches are neglected, they run the risk of not producing fruit. Many of our relationships don't produce the fruit we desire because we are so out of balance. Out-of-balance people neglect those things that are most important—even themselves.

You must take care of yourself and your mate. If your conversations are dominated by worries or concerns only about work or anything or anyone else that threatens to consume you, most likely you need to find balance. You are a person with a lot going on in you and around you, but you are more than a job or a family member, church member, or community member. We are who we are apart from our roles and social expectations. If you have too many things up in the air, if you leave too many loose ends, or if you feel like your marriage is unraveling, we challenge you to set some priorities and establish new boundaries. Listen openly, communicate honestly, and plan deliberately with your spouse. Ask God for help and support as you move forward together. Finding balance will lead you to your destiny and the abundant life Jesus promised.

## Talking Points

1. Balance is a harmonious arrangement or relation of parts within a whole. A whole, healthy lifestyle includes time for work and play, time for self and others. How balanced is your life? Is your life dominated by work, family, kids, friends, something else?

2. On a scale of one to ten (one being low and ten being high), how balanced is your life?

3. What do you do for fun? What do you do as a couple for fun?

4. Brainstorm ways you can get away together for some "us" time. Do you like the idea of finding Sabbath time?

5. Sometimes in marriage, one person cannot give their full 50 percent so the other person has to give more. How often has that happened in your relationship? What do you or can you do to reclaim balance?

6. Are there things you need to change to better manage your lifestyle? What is one thing you can do this week?

7. What is something that you never have to find time to do? What is something that you always have to find time to do?

8. Does your lifestyle reflect your priorities and boundaries? What changes might you make?

## Chapter 7

# Affirmation, Not Intimidation

Before meeting Stephaine, I had prayed about the kind of woman I desired from the Lord. I was quite specific and knew that she would have to be progressive and successful. When I was married to my first wife, I felt that God had elevated us from the lobby of a hotel to the penthouse (metaphorically speaking). When she passed away, I was confident that whoever God sent into my life would have to at least have access to the club level. The lobby is too unpredictable. I wanted someone who could appreciate the trajectory I was on without being intimidated. Considering this fact, I knew that if I ever met this woman, I could not be intimidated by her or by her success.

****

Before meeting Joseph, I also prayed to God for a mate who had an amazing sense of self. In an earlier chapter, I spoke about writing down a list of qualities that I was asking God for in a mate. I wasn't asking for someone who was arrogant or conceited but rather someone who was comfortable in his own skin and not easily intimidated by others and especially not by me—what I did for a living or my potential, either financially or otherwise. Because of prior relationships, I had gotten to the point that I wouldn't tell people what I did for a living out of concern that they might be too intimidated to inquire further. It sounds silly, I know, but it's true; and the fact of the matter is women do this everyday in their quest to find a mate. They make themselves seem "less than" so that they don't scare away potential prospects. But if you make yourself appear "less than," you may fail to recognize that you could end up forcing yourself to deal with situations God never meant for you to have to deal with.

****

If someone is intimidated by you for whatever reason and walks away, that person just did you a favor. By being honest, you are instantly weeding out the people who will have difficulty handling the calling and anointing God has placed on your life. If you fail to be honest, you run the risk of forcing yourself to go through an unnecessary process whereby you waste time, money, thoughts, and feelings only to end up with the same exact result. Because eventually it just won't work. Only instead of taking five minutes of your time, you've taken five weeks, or five months, or even worse, two kids and five years. We say all of this not because we've always had the answers, but because of all of the mistakes we have made. As always, you live and you learn. Never be anything other than the beautifully gifted person God made you to be.

Who in your life makes you feel "less than"? Who in your life makes you feel "more than"? Who lifts you up with encouragement? If you don't have people in your life who encourage and support you, you need to find them. Do you have Christian friends? How might Christian friends make a difference in your life as individuals, as a couple?

No one wants to be in a relationship with a person who intimidates or uses intimidation to get their way. We just want someone who will be accepting of the areas where we need growth and supportive of our strengths and accomplishments. Stephaine and I are no different. I didn't want Stephaine to act weaker just to make me feel more like a man. And I didn't want Joseph to be or act weaker just to make me feel like I was taking care of him. That would be dishonest and bring us down as a couple.

## Joseph's Story

Stephaine is a very accomplished woman. She has degrees from Vanderbilt, Cornell, and Harvard. She is young, beautiful, and powerful in her field, and I see how some men might be intimidated by her. I meet a lot of men who struggle with intimidation. They feel that a woman who is powerful in her own right somehow diminishes who they are. Often I hear men wonder what can they do for a woman like that? When you are confident in who you are, you are not threatened by the success of your mate. God brought you together to complement each other, not to compete with each other.

### *Complement, Not Compete*

I know as you read this you are saying, "Easier said than done." I meet so many people who say that others are intimidated by their success. Women especially deal with men who can't handle them making more money then they do or having more education than they do, and the list goes on and on. On the other hand, I meet men who say women are intimidated by them because of the company they keep and a variety of other reasons. *Relationships of destiny do not develop when there is a spirit of intimidation. They are birthed out of affirmation.* When two progressive people come together, they can both appreciate and affirm what each brings to the table. I could have easily been intimidated by Stephaine, but I realized that our relationship was one of destiny. God knew what kind of woman I needed to be with in order for His will to manifest in our lives.

We all need affirmation, but how affirming are you? Do you go out of your way to encourage your mate? Do you look for things in other people to praise, or do you have to always be the center of attention? I think it's important to emphasize that, in relationships of destiny, couples do not compete with each other, rather they complement each other. God brought us together as a team. When one person on the team is penalized, the entire team is penalized; when one person scores, the team scores. When your mate is doing great things, it blesses your team. What Satan wants to do is divide you, because he knows a house divided against itself cannot stand. This is why it is so important to be on the same team and not be intimidated by each other's gifts. This means you are not divided and that you can speak with the same voice when it comes to dealing with family, friends, commitments, decisions, and priorities.

When we allow intimidation to enter our relationship, it exposes our insecurities. It's at that point that we lose sight of why God brought us together. The Bible says that "iron sharpeneth iron" (Proverbs 27:17). You need a mate who can challenge you to do better. You should desire somebody who refuses to settle for average. *Average is simply being on top of the bottom. God has not called you to be on top of the bottom, rather to be on top of the top.* You are an extraordinary individual, and what God has deposited in you should never be a threat to the person you are in relationship with. The same is true with your mate. Rather than be intimidated by who your mate is, you should offer affirmation and support.

### *Communicate Your Support*

Communicating your affirmation must happen with intentionality. You cannot take this area for granted or think that it will happen without conscious effort, because the temptation in every relationship is an assumption that the other person knows how you feel. This is one reason men, in particular, are not as expressive or thoughtful as most women would like. We often operate out of this assumption and leave our mates confused as to our level of support and commitment to what God is doing in their lives.

I intentionally speak words of affirmation to Stephaine daily. She knows that it comes from a place of sincerity and not redundant routine, because she knows me. When she completes a project or speaks at a function, I remind her how proud I am of her. I recognize that people are calling for her because she has something to say. I embrace her worth and constantly demonstrate my support to her. How do you embrace the worth of your mate? What words of support do you offer? What affirmation does your spouse need to hear directly from you? Try making a list of five ways your spouse makes you proud and find a time today to tell them.

Please understand, if you allow yourself to neglect speaking words of affirmation, your spouse will interpret it as non-support, perhaps rooted in intimidation. Affirming each other is making what's important to your mate a priority in your life. Although I am a pastor and reach millions around the world, there is only one voice, other than Jesus Christ, that I listen to for encouragement. It's Stephaine telling me that she thanks God for me and how God uses me. She knows exactly what to say and, more important, when to say it.

One of the questions that people have asked me is this: Was Stephaine intimidated by what I did and who I was? I understand the context of the question quite well. But my response is, "Not at all." She is quite secure and didn't need what I did to define her. She is perfectly fine in her own skin and that helped her be comfortable with who I am. And we both have learned how to affirm and support each other as we progress in our respective fields.

### *Insecurity Spawns Intimidation*

When people have low self-esteem and struggle with using intimidation, they usually enjoy and seek out relationships with people who are "not at their level." They do this because they are insecure with who they are. What I mean by this is that people who use intimidation love to control others. But they need to control because they feel out of control within their own soul. The controlling spirit manifests itself because they need people to become dependent upon them. They often need power over someone to prove to themselves that they count for something more important than what they feel they are now.

These types of arrangements are not healthy. When a person does not agree with you and has the power to take away your basic needs, that's too much power to give a person. Persons who are insecure with who they are often resort to bullying. Relationships of destiny are not that way; rather, they are spiritual. Relationships of destiny reach for greatness within a person; they seek to lift persons up with humility and generosity. Relationships of destiny seek to put on the mind of Christ and also seek the mind of Christ in the other person. (See 1 Corinthians 2:14-16.)

I was also attracted to Stephaine intellectually. I must admit that her accomplishments were quite appealing because they spoke volumes about who she is as a person. Any person who had achieved what she had would have to be focused, committed, and unwavering in the pursuit of excellence. I knew this would translate in every area of her life. Stephaine is a woman of excellence, and I welcome that because I am a man of excellence. As our youth say, "game recognizes game." Stephaine and I are connected by similar passions and drive. She pushes me, and I push her—using not intimidation but affirmation. This is what makes our relationship work and what keeps us moving toward the fulfillment of destiny.

When God created the institution of marriage it was clear that the spirit of intimidation had no place. God gives the admonition to Adam and Eve to be fruitful and multiply. In order to fulfill this, there must camaraderie between them. Adam would need everything God placed in Eve, and she would need what God placed within him. The goal is clear. They are supposed to walk through the garden fulfilling their destiny. When we understand that what God has deposited in our mates is essential to our own destiny coming to fruition, we will move past issues of intimidation and insecurity. All of us at some level must deal with the demons of insecurity. There is something within us all that causes us to struggle with our sense of worth and significance, but remember that you are on the same team and when one person excels the entire team excels.

### *Love Seeks Good for the Other*

In 1 Corinthians 13:4 Paul shares a powerful word about love. He says that love does not envy. When you love someone, you want to see the best in them. When envy is present you will find yourself harboring resentment and bitterness toward your mate. Love is selfless and seeks the good of the other over your own. Again, "selfless" does not mean "without a self" but rather a self who "thinks of self less and others more." Then, when unchained from our own selfish desires and motives, we can truly celebrate each other. Relationships of destiny must understand and embrace this fact. When we are envious of each other, we rob ourselves of God's best for our lives. I've often said that it is important to have people in your life who don't just tolerate you but who genuinely celebrate you. There are so many amazing things that Stephaine does, and I enjoy celebrating those things with her.

### *We All Need Affirmation*

Let me share more about the need for affirmation. This is an area that many of us take for granted. If your relationship is going to be one moving toward destiny, it's important to affirm each other because affirmation brings with it encouragement. Not long ago, I saw an amazing thing happen at a basketball free throw line. I noticed that the entire team gave a slap to the hand whether the person shooting made the free throw or not. This high five carried a dual meaning. If they made the shot, it meant, "Proud of you!" or "Great shot." If they missed the shot it meant, "No worries, you can make the next one!" Either way the team chose to encourage the player at the line.

I think that it is important to affirm each other whether we have high points or low points in our relationship. When your mate does something awesome, they should feel that you are their number one cheerleader. They should feel your support and know that you are so proud of their accomplishment. If they totally bum out on something, it is important that your words of affirmation are heard as well. They should know that they can overcome this setback and that you are there for them. Words of affirmation lift our spirits and motivate us to achieve in areas where we otherwise would have given up. Knowing I've got someone in my life walking toward destiny and affirming me makes the journey so much easier.

We all need affirmation—some more than others. Whether we admit it or not, affirmation inspires us and gives us that much needed push to excel. One of the things that Stephaine does so well is offer words of affirmation. There is never a day that goes by that we don't affirm each other. When she leaves the house, it is important that she leaves knowing I've got her back and she has my back. Regardless of the things that are going on in our lives, we are very intentional about affirmation.

### *God's Providential Hand*

Paul writes in Romans 8:28: "All things work together for good to them that love God, to them who are the called according to his purpose." We often use this scripture to encourage people who are experiencing a plethora of issues all at the same time. This scripture certainly encourages; however, it also puts in perspective how God providentially works things together in our lives to bless the relationship of destiny. I believe that God works in seasons. He may elevate one of you in your career while the other has to wait. He knows exactly what you can handle and when you can handle it. Ultimately both of you will walk in the purpose and destiny you imagined. Until then, you have to know that God is at work allowing you to learn how to support each other. This season is designed for you to learn to encourage each other. This is an opportunity to work through your insecurities and be the person God has called you to be in your marriage.

When I look back on our relationship, I am totally convinced that God was and is at work in our lives. Stephaine and I recognize that God had to prepare us for not only what He was going to do in our own lives individually but also what He was going to do in the other's life. God knew the temperament, patience, and spirit I would need to be with someone on Stephaine's trajectory. Oftentimes we fail to understand that some people may not be able to navigate at the altitudes where God intends to take us. This is why God releases us from certain relationships early on. Sometimes we resist what God is doing because we want a thing to work out, but God knows the capacity of the person we are with and what he or she can handle. It's not that he or she is not a good person; it's just that some people will always struggle with your level of success.

Imagine this: God knows where we will end up, and He is preparing you all the time for this end. He sits, looking down upon our lives, knowing the paths we will take. Jeremiah 29:11 says, "For I know the thoughts that I think toward you, saith the LORD, thoughts of peace, and not of evil, to give you an expected end." God knows the end. He finishes a thing long before we start a thing. The things that happen in between are necessary to position and prepare us for the destination.

### *Arrive Together at Your Destiny*

When you know that God has your destination in mind, you are willing to fight through the trivial matters that seek to destroy your relationship and push toward destiny together. When you understand that God has this awesome thing He is going to do through both of you, you then can see how issues of intimidation have no place in your relationship. As all things work together for your good, God will make sure that you arrive at your destiny *together*. Though one person may excel at a quicker pace than the other, destiny is something you arrive at together. God will never bless me walking into destiny without Stephaine or her walking in without me. We are tied together in this journey and must affirm each other and not be intimidated by each other. The devil desires to use intimidation as a weapon to stifle your destiny from coming to pass. If I allow intimidation in our marriage, I put a limit on what God desires to do through us both.

****

## Stephaine's Story

As a young single person, I had my share of experiences dealing with people who could not handle the idea that I had a higher level of education, that I was a doctor, or that I was financially independent and potentially might bring home the higher income. Or they might be intimidated by my very close-knit family. These particular qualities quite often brought out the insecurities of the men I dated. This would happen so frequently that it got to the point that from day one, people would pretend to be something or someone they were not and tell elaborate tales of what they were involved in or doing—just to seem more impressive. But they always eventually got tired of pretending and got frustrated at the tangled web of untruths they left in their path. As a result they would either begin to try to diminish my accomplishments or begin to treat me like less of the child of God I knew myself to be, all in order to make them feel better about who they were, or were not for that matter.

Over time, I learned to not take these behaviors personally. When they occurred it did not speak about me or about my character. Instead it shed a great deal of light on the other persons and their insecurities, none of which truly had anything to do with me but rather were simply the result of improperly placed baggage on their part. I could not allow myself to own that.

When Joseph and I met, I had gotten to a point where I had made up in my mind that I could be no one else but myself. So I refused to hide the fact that I was a doctor or pretend that I was less intelligent or less independent. I wanted him to know me right up front, so he could make the choice about whether he felt comfortable or not. I knew instantly he was different. When he first asked what I did and I told him, he was so intrigued. He was so inquisitive. He demonstrated a genuine interest not just in what I did but also in the many things I had yet to do. He too was accomplished and did not feel the least bit threatened. We would talk for hours at a time. It was so refreshing. I was driven. He was driven. We share so many interests and curiosities. I had finally met my intellectual twin, as we like to say. We both recognized that we were both real "nerds." We love bookstores and history and are both consummate learners. And it hasn't stopped.

### *My Biggest Cheerleader*

I can honestly say that in our marriage Joseph is so tremendously supportive of everything I feel called to do, as I am with him. He is my biggest cheerleader, whether what I am doing at the time involves him or not. Joseph absolutely affirms who I am as a woman, a doctor, a philanthropist, a community leader, and a wife. He supports me in my gifts and is not the least bit intimidated by who I am, what I do, or what I bring to the marriage. He believes in me, even when I do not believe in myself. He challenges me intellectually. He will often look at me and see gifts in me that I sometimes don't even see in myself. He helps push me outside of my comfort zone to accomplish things that I never thought I had it in me to do. It is because of Joseph and his unconditional love, support, and continued affirmation that today I am a better me. How do you challenge and act as a cheerleader for your spouse? Is this something that comes easily or do you have to work on it?

### *Going from Good to Great*

I support my husband 110%. I love him and want to see him succeed in everything he is anointed to do. Although we support each other unconditionally, we don't always agree with everything the other person says. Actually, we have regular healthy debates. Do you really want your spouse to tell you that you are right all of the time, even when you are not? We are both firm believers in the fact that iron sharpens iron. *We would rather have someone who can look you in the eyes with love in their heart and tell you when you are wrong or challenge your thoughts so that the implementation of your God-given vision can go from good to great.* We regularly bounce ideas off of each other, not necessarily for affirmation all of the time but because we both know that we will tell each other the truth.

We both do our best to just be present and supportive of each other whenever and however—for both the small things and the large things. For example, whenever I have an event, project, or deadline, he's right there supporting me in every way he can—whether it be momentarily taking care of the household duties so I can focus, proofreading a paper for me, or simply leaving me alone when he sees that's what I need in order to be productive. Whatever it is, he'll do it. Whenever I have to speak somewhere, I can always look up and see Joseph sitting in the audience with a big grin on his face, as if to say, "Now, that's my wife right there!"

He only wants to see me succeed. He is not saying he's supportive and then secretly planning how he can sabotage me so I don't outshine him—no, not at all. Because I'm a person who would prefer to stay in the background, it is Joseph who is often the force encouraging, or even, when necessary, pushing me into the spotlight. But on the flip side, when Joseph has an important event or big speaking engagement, or when it's his time to shine, I am always right behind him or by his side without hesitation or reservation, supporting him in every way that I possibly can.

*Being in the Supporting Role*

However, I do see how there may be the risk of feeling intimidated if you are married to a person who has a relatively high-profile job (not just a pastor but any occupation). One concern may be how you behave in a supportive role, or you may feel that you could be forced to shrink into your spouse's shadow. That was certainly something that Joseph and I openly talked about. He doesn't want me to be seen as just "the pastor's wife." It is important to Joseph that I be seen as much more than that—not because being a pastor's wife is not an honorable role but simply because there's more to me than that. Yes, I am a pastor's wife, and I love supporting my husband and genuinely want to see him succeed and bless the lives of others as he operates in his gifts. However, I also love the other aspects of who I am and what I do.

It is really important to Joseph that he support me in my other endeavors, so that I don't lose the essence of who I am behind his mammoth image. And that's not to say I can prevent myself from being in his shadow at times, because I cannot. But I am more than comfortable with that, because it doesn't define me or my entire existence. In a marriage like this, it's critical to have a very strong sense of self, to be comfortable in your own skin, and to have a spouse who supports you exploring and delving into those things that are important to you.

### *We Succeed Best Together*

With all that we have going on, you might think that we find ourselves competing with each other at times, but that's not the case at all. When he succeeds—we succeed. When I succeed—we succeed. We constantly affirm each other. That's just what we do. I tell Joseph how amazing I think he is, how he makes me a better me. I tell him how important it is for me to see him in the back of the room when I give a talk. I tell him about all the wonderful things he does to make sure that I know without a shadow of a doubt that he respects me, what I do, and what I have to offer our relationship. I tell him these things because I don't want to make the assumption that he knows how important his support is to me. I don't take it for granted. With everything he does, he could be very self-centered, but he is anything but that. Much of the time *he is me-centered and I am him-centered.* That, to us, is what marriage is about. If we can't be supportive of each other, then what's the point? I mean really. I know without a shadow of a doubt if no one else is supportive of me, Joseph is and he will be right by my side.

At the end of the day, when you marry someone, you want that person to be someone who loves you unconditionally. You want someone who supports you in those things you are passionate about; someone who challenges you and encourages you to move beyond your comfort zone to do those things he or she knows you are capable of doing despite the fact that YOU may not feel or believe you can do them; someone willing to be your cheerleader and stand in your corner whether you win or lose; someone who can tell you when you are right, yet someone who's not afraid to look you in the face to tell you when you are wrong.... That's what you want. Our covenant is that we succeed best together.

****

## THE CUP AND SAUCER PARABLE

ONE OF THE MOST IMPORTANT THINGS that we need to do on an individual basis is be confident in our gifts and talents and know that we bring something significant to the relationship. You are important, and regardless of whose season it is to "shine," it's essential that you approach success as a united front. Here is a cup and saucer analogy. Someone asked the saucer one day if it was tired of always holding up the cup. He was concerned that the saucer would never have its day but always be servant to the cup. After a series of questions, the saucer responded with a simple answer, "I'm fine being a saucer. Whenever the cup runs over, I get the overflow." Sometimes you have to be the saucer while the other person is the cup. The other person will get the attention, pouring out and being used while the saucer is often unseen and viewed as insignificant. The blessing of the saucer is that it thrives on the success of the cup, because what's in the cup flows into the saucer. In our marriage, when one of us is blessed, the other is also blessed. Neither of us minds being a seasonal saucer, especially when we know the cup will overflow often.

## GOD PREPARES FOR YOUR DESTINY

GOD'S WILL FOR YOUR MARRIAGE is that you support each other. One of the worst feelings in any relationship is feeling a lack of support. If you are single, it's important to know that right now God is preparing you to support an incredible person, and He's preparing that person to support you too. It's not just about where you are now: it's about where you are going. When He brings you together, it will always be the right time. If we had met a year earlier, we might not have been ready to walk toward destiny together. Our lives were so complicated individually that we probably would have viewed anything outside of what we were doing as a threat. God knew when we were ready for each other. We both are people who resist complacency at all cost. We focus on what God is doing in our lives. And now we recognize that whatever He is doing in our life individually will influence us collectively. We both know how to decrease so the other can increase. We get it. It's not about being intimidated by each other; it's about affirming each other. Take a moment and think about how God prepared you before you met your mate.

## GOING TO THE NEXT LEVEL

WHEN YOU RECOGNIZE WHAT Paul says in Philippians 2:13, it will take your relationship to the next level. "It is God which worketh in you both to will and to do of his good pleasure." Remember, God is at work, and He's up to something through you both. You are a part of a relationship of destiny. Every day when you wake up, think of ways to affirm each other. This journey is difficult and can be quite lonely. It will take both of you to make this thing happen. You were born to support each other. You are destined to make it together.

## Talking Points

1. Talk together about how God is working in your life now.

2. Life is a spiritual journey with a beginning, middle, and end. Where are you on your journey as an individual and as a couple?

3. When one of you succeeds, both succeed. Take a moment and each share one of your biggest successes. Who was there? Who encouraged you? Who was not there who you might have wished had been there? What does it still mean to you?

4. Do you share and celebrate your successes as a couple?

5. Since we are born to support each other, name three ways you support your spouse. What are some ways that you can show your support even better?

6. Promise each other that you will find new ways to be encouraging and supportive. Also promise that you will accept the other person's affirmation.

7. Make a list of the things you want to accomplish in the next year; next five years; next ten years.

Chapter 8

# Space and Grace

Forever is a long time. When you are seriously dating, engaged, or married, it is important to understand this reality. Marriage is a covenant that is meant to last forever, but making a covenant and keeping your covenant can be two different things. Marriage grows out of a commitment to love, cherish, and keep each other, but being married is meant not to bind you but to liberate you and lead you to destiny. And part of abiding in your marriage commitment is growing in grace to give your spouse space so that you both will thrive.

## Joseph's Story

Many folks have unrealistic views. We hear couples say, "I want to spend every moment with my loved one." Although this is admirable, it is not realistic. Whether you know it or not, you will need space from each other in order to reflect, regroup, and revive yourself so that you can pour back into the relationship. We call this space and grace. It takes a great deal of grace to release your loved one to a place where they can have some time away from you, whether it be with friends or family. This grace allows adequate space so that you don't crowd each other out. This does not mean that you don't do things together.

Stephaine and I do most all things together, but we've also come to a place where we understand how important space and grace are to the longevity of our relationship.

I remember the day Stephaine and I came to a roadblock. Women, men need to be around men for competition and fellowship. Without this we become discontent. It took a while for Stephaine to understand this. I needed to go play ball alone. I needed to go visit my friends in other cities from time to time because of the nature of our careers. As professional colleagues, we need to vent and encourage one another. Often those one-day trips feel like weeks of relaxation, because I don't have the pressures from church hovering over me. But Stephaine felt that we should do these things together, and I understood her point. Couples should share together; however, there are times when you just need space. After much discussion and understanding, she granted me the grace to walk in my own space from time to time. You cannot overcrowd your mate and not allow them space to breathe apart from you, because at the end of the day, they are coming home to you.

When examining this area candidly, you might uncover some insecurities that have carried over from previous relationships. This is the baggage we discussed earlier. A lot of couples struggle with giving space out of fear of what might happen within that space. This is the elephant in the room. Trust issues are huge in relationships and often result in one mate becoming overly clingy. This is something that will erode the relationship and create unnecessary stress. You must fight that temptation and move beyond your insecurities to allow your mate to have some needed freedom.

Take a moment and think about these things: how easy or difficult is it for you to give your mate space? Can you talk openly about this as a couple? What does giving space really mean to you? Consider your motives for giving or not giving space. Are you afraid that your spouse might leave you? Are you jealous that the other person can do something you won't or can't? Did you just grow up that way? Perhaps you are just unaware how much or little space your mate needs? What makes you feel "crowded" in your relationship? Are you losing sight of your destiny because your mate feels crowded out?

### *Destiny Demands Alone Time*

Jesus Christ walked with twelve men in a strategic relationship of destiny. Even though He was committed to the assignment of training them, He also took time away to talk to His Father. Jesus went away to pray alone. This space was necessary in order for Him to refuel, so that He could be more effective in His relationships. If Jesus needed space, you and your mate do as well. Space in relationship is essential so that you can both reflect and feel renewed. Relationships take work. They require daily attention. If you are not refueling, you are going to run out of gas.

When we talk about space, it's not always about being in separate physical places far from each other. Stephaine and I have learned something about each other. We have developed our ways of giving space within the house. I retreat to my office, and she works, reads, and reflects sitting on the bed. It's unspoken in our home when we need this space. It's just a given. When I go into my office, it's not always about work. I am surfing the web, going between YouTube and Google. I am watching sporting events from my office as well. It's my space. It's that hour or so during the day that I need to just reconnect with me. She does the same in her space. The deeper issue here is reconnecting with yourself and with God. You have to have those moments where you center. Those moments are where you reflect upon where you are in life and where the relationship is, and where you just talk to God. To Stephaine's credit, she seldom invades this space. It is necessary for me to have it, and she recognizes that when I come out of it, I can then be totally focused on her.

### *Giving Space Creates Relational Grace*

The fear for many couples is that space means they no longer get attention. Actually, you will get more attention if you allow your mate to have space. There are a variety of things you will be doing together—most things to be exact. Giving your mate the grace of space means you have come to understand what that space creates within your relationship. You see how it benefits what you already have. Whether it's basketball, golf, the office, or a trip with the guys, men need a little space. I speak for the men primarily, because I've had to explain to many couples why this is so important for men.

### *From the Man's Perspective*

But before I go any further, let me say that I recognize that generalizations are not healthy. I only speak from my context and the numerous conversations I have had with men who desire space. When a man enters into a committed relationship, there are a whole host of things he has to overcome. He may deal with the guys making fun of him for throwing away the "little black book." He may deal with breaking generational curses, because most of the men in his family have not been the men God desired them to be. He may struggle with whether he can live up to what God expects of him. He even may be referred to in the past tense. You might hear someone say this about a groom, "You remember Keith, don't you? He's married now." They say this as though he is gone.

The way we as men are socialized is completely different; so when we commit, we really want to be committed. Now, the other side of this is that space for a man gives him some level of normalcy. If that space is taken from him, he rebels and feels trapped. He begins to feel as though his life is being controlled by the relationship and he is a prisoner in his own home. Privately, this enrages him and causes him to look for ways to escape. The devil will use this desire to manipulate him in ways inconsistent with God's will.

I've seen numerous men in situations like this: men who enter the relationship with great expectations but are frustrated by mates who they perceive as too clingy. It makes men want to walk away. This is why it's so important to understand the need men have for space.

### *Women Need Space Too*

Women need space as well. They need space to stay connected to their girlfriends, who play a significant role in their lives. I've seen Stephaine on the phone for hours with a friend. They may not talk every day, but when they do talk, they catch up on so much, and it gives Stephaine such a great feeling. I see what space does for her, and I embrace it and affirm the need for it.

### *The Divine Power of Space*

I'm sure as some of you read this book, negative thoughts about space and grace might come to your mind. Thoughts like "If they need space, why don't they stay single?" Married or single, we all need space. It's a part of life. Don't underestimate the divine power of space, because God can work through space to transform our lives and deliver us back to the relationship as much better people.

In the book of Genesis, Jacob was left alone and wrestled with a messenger from God until the break of day. Through this experience Jacob was changed and even given a new name to commemorate his struggle. It's in moments when we are alone that God deals with us in those private areas of our lives. Make no mistake about it. Space involves recreation, but it also involves contemplation. On one hand, we can have fun with Christian friends; but on the other hand, we can be in position to hear God's voice without the music of our relationship playing.

Each year I go away alone to hear from God so that I can be clear on the direction God wants to take the church in the following year. At first it was difficult explaining to Stephaine why I needed to go alone. From her perspective, she felt that just being there would not be a problem. Although it's never a problem when my wife is present, I explained to her that I love her so much that her presence would distract me and naturally cause me to pour into her. I needed this time for God to pour into me. I needed this time to hear clearly what God was saying to His people. So often we want to know what God is saying to us regarding our relationships but we don't put ourselves in position to hear Him.

### *Being Sensitive about Giving Space*

One of the most important things that Stephaine helped me with is telling me what she needs. Relationships of destiny require us to be sensitive to what both people need in the relationship. Stephaine indicated that she needed to feel secure while I was in my space. If I was going to be away, it was important for her to always have access to me. This is a level of accountability that is necessary for space to be granted. Because my intentions were right in requesting space, this was easy to grant. If you struggle with giving complete access while in your own space, you may want to evaluate your motives. The fact that she knows where I'm staying and knows my phone will be on at all times gives her that extra added security in the relationship. *It's not a trust thing; it's a security thing.* She needs to feel covered. If she needs me for anything, she knows I'm there. With the advances of technology, I have now begun to Skype with her while I'm away. We do this each night before I go to bed. This holds me accountable and allows me the opportunity to give my wife the security she needs and deserves.

It is helpful to our relationships to ask our mates what their needs are when granting space. I don't criticize Stephaine for expressing her needs or get angry, rather I affirm how she feels and comply. So often we trivialize our mates' needs by rebuking them for sharing. Even though space is necessary in the relationship, it is a huge step to undertake and should be seen as such. This is something that requires a great deal of faith and trust. We must communicate with each other our true feelings and be honest about why we need what we need.

### *Be Covered in Prayer*

Allow me to give a word of warning. The devil will always attempt to challenge you in the space area. When we are alone Satan uses this isolation to begin his interrogation of us. He begins to call your integrity into question and will present you options to fill that space since your mate is not there. That's why it's important to be covered in prayer and take nothing for granted. Remember, Jesus was in the wilderness alone when Satan tempted Him, but He had been fasting and praying and was ready for the battle. You cannot take this moment of space at a time when you are worn down and not built up in your faith. Satan will use this weakness to discredit your Christian witness. Every day, Stephaine and I pray that God will cover us both. We know the devil is busy and desires to destroy what God has put together. We are committed to covering our marriage in prayer. We refuse to give the devil a place in that space.

I used this illustration once while preaching and it made the point. If my wife cooks a great meal and serves the finest entrée and dessert, I will be full when I leave home. When I leave home I will pass several restaurants along the path of my destination. Though they are fine restaurants, I am not tempted because I was completely full when I left home. This illustration is clear. Because my needs are met within the marriage and I am covered in prayer, what might be a challenge for me is not an issue. Again I say take nothing for granted in your marriage. Make sure you are doing what you need to do before space is granted. When I'm in that space, I am focused on spiritual things and not things of the flesh.

Every relationship will come to this point. We will all desire those moments when we can do things apart from the relationship itself. It's important for the other person to know that it is not a reflection upon the state of the relationship; rather, it is a natural evolution of things. The relationship can be healthy and vibrant and still need space. You must not digress into believing that the person is no longer happy or needs something else. That has nothing to do with it. It's about being able to pour back into each other. Stephaine and I jokingly say that we give space so we can "really" miss each other. This adds spark to our marriage. It adds creativity to our marriage. Absence really does make the heart grow fonder.

There are a lot of things that you enjoy doing that should not be lost in your relationship. Couples should understand the need for these things in maintaining what I call relational sanity. I use this term because I've counseled people who have become frustrated because their mate crowded them. I need to say simply that it's OK to give your mate space. Once you've agreed on the terms, it should be an easy thing to do. Even as Stephaine and I write this book, we are doing it in our own space. Although we spend significant time together, I needed this space to reflect upon our relationship so that I could write freely. Many couples miss out on wonderful creative opportunities because space is not valued.

### *The Importance of Presence and Availability*

God desires our relationships to be fruitful and enjoyable. This is why He allowed you and your mate to come together in the first place. Relationships of destiny are those where God gives us the grace to understand each other's needs. Both Stephaine and I realize that we have the gift of grace to allow each other space. Consider the impact of not giving someone the space they need. They will continue to seek it anyway and begin to withdraw from the relationship. When you are in a relationship of destiny, you are present emotionally, physically, and spiritually. There is never a disconnection because you approach each moment refreshed and revived. Whether or not you realize it, your mate can detect if you are there or if you are absent; likewise, it is incredibly frustrating when a person constantly needs space and can't get it.

****

## Stephaine's Story

In our marriage, I think giving space was the most challenging thing for me. By now, you know that without a shadow of a doubt I love my husband. Although our schedules are hectic, we go out of our way to set aside time to spend with each other. When we were courting, because we were in a long-distance relationship, whenever we were in the same city we were inseparable. Where he was, I was. Where I was, he was. No questions needed. But fast-forward to after we married when I began to see things abruptly change. With us now living together in the same city, same home, being together "now and forever 'til death do us part," I began to see differences in Joseph's behavior.

On one hand, I had just moved to Nashville. Almost right away, though, he was back to his regular routine: playing basketball with friends in the mornings, going into the church to work in his office there, running errands alone, then returning home in the early evening. At first, I just thought it was a fluke, and then I realized it was becoming a pattern. That's clearly a normal pattern for most couples, but because this was such a drastic change from our premarital days, I was concerned. After speaking to Joseph, I had a revelation. He was resuming the "marital routine" that he once knew. I had to explain to him that I loved spending time with him. However, he expressed that based on his previous experience, he had come to learn that in marriage it is imperative to give each person their own time and space, so that's what he was trying to do. But since we had just gotten married, I wasn't quite on that page yet and frankly felt it difficult to adapt.

Although he had previously been married, I had not. I had to explain to Joseph that our time together during this transition was still sacred to me, and I wasn't prepared to let it go. At the time, I honestly couldn't understand what the big deal was. I had grown up in a family where my parents have been married now going on fifty years and they are still seemingly joined at the hip. He seemed to understand at the time, and it wasn't long before I found us right back to spending time together as I preferred.

### *How Much Togetherness Is Too Much?*

As I became more acclimated to the area and as our life together began to pick up pace, we began to be pulled in every direction imaginable. Despite the fact that our free time was dwindling, Joseph came up to me one day and said, "I love you, but I really need to go away to spend time with my friends." At first it felt like an arrow through the heart. All I could think of was, "But wait; recently we haven't had any time to spend together, and now the little bit of free time we have you want to take to hang out with your friends? How can you do this to me?" Yes, sadly, that's how I felt at the time. I know, NOW I'm embarrassed about it. But I really did feel justified at the time.

This is one thing that has taken me almost two years to understand, and although I am certain that I still do not fully comprehend it, I now at least understand how it affects Joseph and our marriage. Granted, most people have a very tight circle of close friends. For both Joseph and me, few, if any, of our closest friends are nearby. Almost everyone lives out of state. Not to say that we don't have friends in Nashville. We certainly do, and we love them and spend time with them as well when we can. But most of us understand what it means to have friends who have been through it all with you and know you just as well as you know yourself. The only time we tend to see our closest friends is when we are traveling either for work or for other ministry-related events. So although we get an opportunity to see them, it's usually brief and short-lived.

For my girlfriends and me, because we've spent most of our time in separate cities, when we see each other it's wonderful; but when we don't, we understand. Since all of us have demanding careers, it's not a big deal. Some are married and others even have children and have to deal with related life responsibilities. So we just pick up wherever we leave off when we have a chance to catch up. Of course, I miss my friends, and it's not ideal to not be able to see or talk to them regularly, but 'tis life. Right? Well, so I thought, until I got married. I slowly came to realize that, for Joseph, although he faced similar challenges as I did, they influenced him in a completely different way. In all seriousness, what I've come to learn being married to my husband is that, for men, spending time with men and the whole male-bonding thing seems to be a part of their genetic makeup. To deny them this is to deny them being a man. For whatever reason, it's a much bigger deal for him if he does not get an opportunity to hang out with other guys. It's a "dude thing," he always says.

I do know that one reason is because, as a pastor and spiritual leader, it's difficult to find friends who will look at him as an equal and true friend—not as their pastor. So the friends who have stood by him over the years through thick and thin provide friendships that he not only cherishes but genuinely needs. They keep him both grounded and rejuvenated. I used to protest in both big and small ways to Joseph traveling for "guys only" trips. I would always ask, "But why can't I go?" I would suggest that I'd just stay in the hotel, go to the spa, work in the room, or go shopping. I could never really understand why he would usually just end up taking a deep breath and saying, "Never mind." My feelings were always so hurt. But what I failed to realize was that my husband needed time for himself away from me. Not because he didn't love me or wanted to GET AWAY, but because there's a certain rejuvenating power that his male buddies can give him that I as his wife simply cannot. Again, I don't pretend to understand completely. But once I saw it for myself, I too was a believer.

Another point of contention was the fact that my husband gets up at o'dark-thirty in the morning at least two or three times a week to play basketball with a large group of guys at the YMCA. Before we got married, the only thing Joseph demanded—and yes, I would say demanded—was that he was still going to play basketball in the gym in the mornings. Of course, under my breath I was saying, "No, you're not," but clearly I lost that battle. There's something about their need to bond on the basketball court. Some men go even when they are hurt and don't even play. They just sit on the sideline and watch ... and bond. There is no way I would get up before the sun to sit on the side of a basketball court just to chat. There's just no way. But therein lies the difference. I've spoken to many of the guys, and they all say the same thing. It's not just about the basketball. Although basketball is what likely brought them together, that's not what's kept them waking up in the morning, some for the last nine to ten years. It's the ability to be around other men to joke, laugh, talk about life, and, yes, play *some* basketball. Needless to say, I have learned to give my husband that, to not fuss when he gets up early in the morning and makes all kind of noise getting ready to go despite the fact that I don't have to get up for hours! I realize that it gives him what I can't—a place for him to bond with other guys.

When I began to understand better what Joseph's needs were and finally stopped putting up such a fuss, it was wonderful. He went to hang out with his best friend in Houston, and when he came back it was like he was a different person. He thanked me for trusting him enough to let him go. But I had to explain to him that it had very little to do with trust because I pray for God to cover and put a hedge around our marriage daily, not just when he goes out of town, so I had no reason to not trust him. I believe our marriage is in God's hands no matter where we are. I went on to tell him that most of my reaction was due to the fact that I just genuinely didn't understand how integral visiting

Our marriage is in God's hands no matter where we are.

those friends was to his life. With this I learned even more about marriage: the fact that if you wish to spend time apart, it doesn't reflect on the love you have for the other person, especially since you both have vowed to spend the rest of your lives together.

One main issue was that Joseph didn't have the heart to tell me early on in our marriage that he needed time and space away. He thought if he came out and said that, he would hurt my feelings. He was right: he would have. Nevertheless, it was something that he needed to say because honestly I was clueless. I had no frame of reference for male bonding. I have my best female friends, and if I see them, that's great. If I don't, it's OK because they know I love them and we will simply pick up where we left off when we talk or see each other again. That's how it's been for years. If we need one another, we are there without hesitation. We speak around the holidays, birthdays, and other big events. Otherwise, life keeps us busy. So I had no frame of reference. I just didn't understand what the big deal was. But for men, for whatever reason, it seems to be different.

Now, two years into our marriage, I look back and realize where he was early on in our marriage. He was clearly miles ahead of me. Although at that time so early in our marriage, I was not prepared for such "separation anxiety," now I am keenly aware that Joseph was correct in the sense that when two people are married, both of you absolutely do need to have your own space and time for yourselves. It is unfair to bring in preconceived notions of what that looks like. It's imperative that the two of you work together to define what that means for your marriage. Now, as time permits, Joseph manages to get away once every couple of months or so to meet up with friends, and it's awesome. To see him so excited to reunite with buddies makes me happy to now be the type of spouse who understands the importance of space and grace. It's been a long time coming, but I'm there now. We have both found that it is very healthy for our marriage to spend some time away with ourselves, or with our respective families or friends, because it allows us to be reenergized while at the same time giving us a chance to miss each other. In the end, ironically, we find that it actually brings us closer together.

****

## EXPRESSING YOUR NEED FOR SPACE

MANY OF YOU READING THIS BOOK need to have a serious conversation with your mate about each other's need for space. These conversations are not easy, because they can conjure up a series of unhealthy emotions and thoughts. If your relationship is going to have longevity, however, you must be willing to work through this area. It's a tough conversation, but it's necessary to the survival of your relationship. We remember the very moment we had this conversation. It was revealing, but it helped us take our marriage to another level. Now we appreciate giving each other space, and it has truly enriched our marriage. We've always missed each other when we were apart, but now we miss each other in ways we never imagined. When either of us returns, it rekindles the fire in our marriage. It allows to us to be creative in showing each other how much we love and miss each other.

Allowing space says to your mate that you affirm their need to reconnect with themselves. It says that you value their needs without judging them or calling their loyalty to the relationship into question. It truly endears them to you and allows them greater opportunity to demonstrate their commitment to you. What an awesome opportunity in relationships.

When you get married, you make a commitment to spend the rest of your life with your mate. Imagine how long that is. Every day you are reminded of that covenant. Every day you will come home to the same person. What a wonderful thought it is to share your life with someone you love completely. It is even more wonderful when you recognize the need to break the routine and position yourself to add spice to the relationship. This is what makes your relationship unique. This is what allows you to be a couple of destiny. You cannot be naïve in your relationship and live under the illusion that you should live every second of every minute in the presence of your mate. This will quickly become problematic in your relationship. Give yourself and your mate an opportunity to breathe and reflect, and it will return huge dividends. Remember, space is only possible when you convey your God-given grace.

## Talking Points

1. Do you like to be alone? If so, what do you like to do by yourself? How much time alone do you need each day? each week? Is there a special place that you like to go for alone time?

2. Are there times in your relationship when you feel smothered? Share an example with your spouse and discuss how it could have been handled differently by both of you.

3. How important is it to have time with your guy or girl friends without your spouse? What do you like to do with your friends? Do you like each other's friends? Why or why not?

4. What would you think if your spouse had lunch with a person of the opposite sex for business reasons only?

5. Does your mate have full access to you, even at work, for emergencies? What counts as an emergency? How can you satisfy your mate's concern for safety?

6. How do you communicate to your spouse that you need some alone time?

7. Are you the kind of person who draws your energy or recharges your battery primarily from being with other people or from being alone? Share a time about when you needed to recharge and how you did it.

## Chapter 9

# Establishing Order in Life's Chaos

One of the most amazing things about God is how He made the world. He literally moved in the midst of chaos and brought order. When you are busy and involved in a lot of things at one time, it's important that you find a system that works for you. As we shared earlier, it is important that you and your mate develop a system of survival. We have chosen to do what's easiest for us. We are not governed by what others think we should do; rather, we have developed a working model that helps us live, despite our chaotic schedules, with some degree of order. Chaos is a part of life, and so often people allow it to frustrate them. While you can't always control the things that happen in life, you can control how you choose to respond to them.

Couples of destiny are progressive. That means they are on the move, heading with deliberate purpose in the direction God is calling them. They seek to maximize moments and seize opportunities. Because of this, life is a series of converging issues, which may seem chaotic at times, despite the many electronic devices that manage our day-to-day activities. It is a continual challenge trying to make sense of life. What makes this interesting is that when you and your mate come together, your lives converge within the chaos that you bring to your relationship.

Managing chaos is a continual work in progress. Just when we think we've figured it out, something else gets added to our schedule and we are thrown off kilter and find ourselves trying to get back to that place where we once had a rhythm. We often say our life is really just "ordered chaos." We know it. We embrace it. We don't try to fight it or change it. It is what it is. It's like looking into the back of a huge grandfather clock. You open the back and what do you see? Numerous small parts. Many don't look like they even match. But when you take a closer look, you can see that a number of them are interconnected and in order for one to move the others have to be operating as well. When everything is working as it should, all of the pieces are moving at the same time. Perhaps even in different directions. It may take you a little while to make sense of all of the interworkings and connections, but eventually you realize that there really is a method to the madness and all of the pieces are necessary components for the clock to work properly.

Our life is a lot like all of the small interworking pieces—networked together—which from the outside look completely unrelated and downright chaotic at times. However, if you spend enough time with us or observe us long enough, you begin to see that we actually do have a cadence to how we operate within our marriage. What is your life like? Is it a well-oiled machine, or does it feel like something is always about to fly off? Does it feel like it is well crafted, or does it feel like everything could come unglued at any moment? Or is it something in between?

## Joseph's Story

I remember walking through New York City and hearing the Lord speak to me. There were tens of thousands of people moving through the hustle and bustle of Manhattan. Although it looked chaotic, there was order within it. And here God reminded me that, although the people I saw changed from day to day, there were still constants. The subway system, yellow cabs, and numerical street names—all of these and more—came together to make the system an integrated whole. These are the things that bring structure and order to folks' lives and allow them to get to their destinations. When you establish consistent and systematic order in your marriage, you have a better chance of not being overwhelmed by the chaos that surrounds you.

Here is an example from my life. On a recent Sunday, I was up at 5:00 a.m. and arrived at church at 6:30 a.m. to preach the first of four services, beginning at 7:00 a.m. After preaching the four services, I was called to the hospital to pray with a member whose mother was dying. I left the hospital at 7:30 that evening and boarded a flight, arriving on the east coast at 6:00 Monday morning. Once I concluded ministering that night, I boarded a plane on Tuesday morning to preach in a midwestern city that night. During the day (Tuesday), I made a series of conference calls and personal calls to members. After the services on Tuesday night, I was on a Wednesday 6:00

a.m. flight back to Nashville to preach three Bible studies. After the noon Bible study, I was in an executive council meeting from 1:30 to 4:00 p.m. After the 5:00 p.m. and 7:00 p.m. Bible studies, I headed home. Thursday, I had two hospital visitations and a funeral. Thursday night, I was scheduled to stop by choir rehearsal to meet with the choir. Friday was supposed to be open; however, I had to go by and pray for a member who was on trial and then meet with the mayor for lunch. I'm sure you are as weary reading this as I was meeting this schedule. That's my schedule; what about yours? Is your schedule pretty much routine or is it different every day?

The ministry is satisfying, helpful, and needed; however, I just want to give you a glimpse of how chaotic my weeks can be. In addition, in the midst of all of this, there is preparation and prayer time for next Sunday's and Wednesday's messages. My days are full and very long. They often look chaotic because of the various things I have to navigate. I love it. I love what I do. But I've had to accept this chaotic and unpredictable schedule as a way of life. When you consider my life and place Stephaine's life in the mix, life gets more complicated. Her schedule is just as demanding. It took us nearly a year to figure out a calendar system to merge our schedules.

The chaos that life brings is a part of any relationship. You don't have to have the same schedule that we do to understand this point. We all understand chaos on a personal level. Your life is speeding along when you hit an unexpected bump—you get sick, the lawnmower breaks, someone hits your car, your spouse loses a job. What we have to understand is that chaos presents itself in unforeseen ways, and it is extremely important that you have a system that governs it so that chaos does not overwhelm you and cause unnecessary tension in your relationship.

### *The Chaos of Personal Storms*

Business can make your life chaotic, but sometimes chaos can manifest itself as personal storms. Being obedient to God does not exempt you from storms in your life. In Mark 4, there is a story of Jesus and His disciples on a ship. Jesus had been teaching by the Sea of Galilee about the seed and the sower. He then instructs the disciples to get into the ship so that they can go to the other side of the sea. Jesus gets in the ship with them but heads to the back of it and promptly goes to sleep. Though the trip begins smoothly, it is soon interrupted by dark skies and a fierce storm. This storm even challenges the expertise of the disciples, some of whom were fisherman by trade. Once they realize this storm is beyond their ability to sail, they begin to panic and call out to Jesus, who is still asleep. When Jesus wakes up, He rebukes their lack of faith and speaks to the storm, "Peace, be still" (Mark 4:39). This story reveals so much to each of us about the chaos in our lives.

Jesus knew that the storm would come; therefore, He tried to prepare the disciples by teaching them prior to getting on the ship. Their faith was weak because they were not paying attention. If you are going to handle the unexpected chaos that will inevitably come in your relationship, you cannot take for granted the importance of getting a Word from God prior to it. Faith comes by hearing, and hearing by the Word of God. If the disciples' faith had been awake, they could have gone to sleep too. Storms will always come in our lives. Many of those storms will be greater than our abilities and expertise. But because you know this, you and your mate can prepare and build yourselves up in the Word so that you don't panic when storms come.

But if you are unprepared and do panic, you bring another level of tension into the relationship. Imagine the chaos on that ship when the storm came. God never allows us to go through things without giving us an opportunity to prepare for that thing before it comes. If you miss this principle, you will bring another level of chaos into a situation where God never intended to frustrate you. Are you prepared? Are you regularly reading the Scriptures and opening yourself to God's teaching? Where do you need God's peace in your life? How good are you about inviting Jesus into your boat?

## *Ordering Chaos in the Midst of Storms*

When Jesus speaks peace to the storm, He is not just managing the chaos, He is transforming it. The disciples are in awe and declare, "What manner of man is this, that even the wind and the sea obey him?" (Mark 4:41). Jesus took authority over the chaos and taught the disciples how to survive within it. When storms come in your life and threaten your relationship, you must remember the power of the Word of God and your ability to speak peace over your situation. This is how you order chaos.

There have been numerous storms in our relationship, so Stephaine and I have developed a system of speaking God's Word over them when they come. *Although we can't control storms, we can control how we respond to them.* Without God's Word we would begin lashing out at each other. This is always an indicator that you need to build yourself up more in the Word of God. When the Word of God becomes important in your relationship, you begin to spend time together reading it and applying it to every chaotic situation that comes. The Word brings order where there is chaos.

### *The Chaos of Demanding Jobs*

Another way chaos manifests in our relationships is through the demands of our careers. As I mentioned earlier, Stephaine and I have demanding schedules, and often it is difficult to adjust them because one thing changes the next thing. Though it may sound quite simplistic, we order this chaos merely by giving everything a place in our schedule. The more the two of you progress in your careers, the more you will appreciate this. Stephaine and I placed a calendar on the wall in our home office, and whenever something is added in either one of our jobs, we post it on that calendar. We have also synchronized our phones and iPads so that when items are added to my calendar, hers is automatically updated. The same happens on her end as well. This simple system helps us order life so that we aren't bumping heads and creating conflicts of schedule that could potentially be problematic up the road.

You and your mate can be intentional about coordinating your calendars. Not only does it mean you are informed but you also are in a position to be accountable to each other. The last thing I want is for Stephaine to be asked where I am and her not know or vice versa.

When you develop this kind of system, it becomes a part of your life and allows you to function more normally in the midst of chaos. People often comment on how Stephaine and I are so even-keeled in light of the demands of our schedules. There is not any way this could happen unless we were intentional about ordering our chaos. My friend and mentor Gordon McDonald has an amazing book entitled *Ordering Your Private World*. One of the most powerful lessons of this book for me has been what he discusses in chapter 7. He calls it "Recapturing My Time." Here are four of his principles that have been especially helpful to me:

1. Unseized time flows toward my weakness.
2. Unseized time comes under the influence of dominant people in my world.
3. Unseized time surrenders to the demands of all emergencies.
4. Unseized time gets invested in things that gain public acclamation.

Gordon stresses the importance of recapturing your time. If you don't capture your time and take control of it, it will certainly take control of you. This is what causes conflict in so many relationships. The inability to order inevitable chaos and manage time effectively will create frustrations that will seep into your relationship and adversely influence it.

### *The Witness of Ordering Chaos*

God continues to give us amazing opportunities to be witnesses for Him through our relationships. How we order chaos is one of them. The devil would love nothing more than to take this opportunity to bless the chaos of the world and make it an obstacle for you and your mate. Every morning you wake up, you should make sure that your life is in order, so that you can be productive amidst the chaos you might encounter throughout the day. If your life is not in order, you will succumb to the chaos and fail to have a fruitful relationship. Structured lives are really a sign that you are focused on the goal. When you and your mate are focused on destiny, it's easy to eliminate anything that poses a threat to where God is taking you. You value time and realize that each moment must be managed carefully in order for you to be productive. Each day is a gift from God, and we must be good stewards of the time God gives us. People who are progressive don't have time to waste. They are passionate about purpose and destiny, and desire people in their lives who share similar thoughts. This is one of the many things Stephaine and I appreciate about each other. We both value time and see the benefits of ordering it.

### *Pacing and Cadence*

Not everyone handles business, storms, or demanding schedules the same way, so one of the things that I encourage every couple to do is to learn each other's cadence. There are times when Stephaine and I are stretched and weary, but because we understand each other, we know what the proper reaction should be in every situation. There are times we are working together, and we both know we are crashing. Interestingly enough, it usually happens around the same time. We know when to step away and put things back in order so that we can maintain productivity. God placed you together to strengthen and encourage each other.

There are times when people will ask Stephaine about my availability to participate in certain functions and events. Because she is aware of my schedule and my cadence, she knows whether I am going to do it or not. I am quite aware of the things that she will do as well. We both guard our schedules and don't allow other people to control them. If you aren't careful, you will allow others to control your schedule and diminish the time you and your mate have together. Life will always pull on you. As long as you have something to contribute, there will never be a shortage of opportunities. You have to determine what makes sense in your world and be content with that. I used to feel guilty saying no to certain requests, but the more I have progressed in life, the more I have realized the need to order the chaos in my life.

### *Step Back and Regroup*

Many of you reading this book are inundated with all the things going on in your life. Your career, children, and the demands of everyday life are taking their toll on you. This may be a good time to step back and regroup. Develop a plan that allows you to maximize your time and bring structure to your life. Can you organize household chores differently? Can you communicate changes better? Don't allow yourself to wallow in frustration. You will never be as productive as God intends if you function out of disorder.

Bishop Paul Morton says, "When a soda machine breaks down, you put an 'Out of Order' sign on it." He talks about this in the context of his own personal experience. When the mind seeks to reign over the things of the spirit, there will always be disorder. Like that soda machine, people will continue to invest in you, expecting you to pour out, but you are unable because there is something wrong. You never want disorder to threaten your destiny. Allow the Sprit to reign over your mind. Don't allow your mind to convince you that you can function in disorder and chaos without a plan. God has always had a plan to bring order to chaos, and He intends us to have one as well.

Your relationship of destiny is designed to bear fruit.

Your relationship of destiny is designed to bear fruit. It is designed for the glory of God in the earthly realm. Stephaine and I realize that God brought us together for purposes far greater than us. We work daily on establishing order in our individual lives as well as our life together. But just because you develop a system of order doesn't mean it cannot change. You will encounter numerous challenges in your life. Your relationship will constantly experience chaotic situations; however, you must see them not as obstacles but as opportunities to show the world how to order chaos. You must be willing to implement strategies that work for the both of you—and to change those strategies as needed. In a real sense, you are making life less stressful.

****

## Stephaine's Story

To be quite honest, it has taken a bit of time to get where we are. Ordering the chaos in our lives definitely didn't happen overnight. It was a journey, with a LOT of trial and error. One of the most pivotal decisions Joseph and I ever made together was related to how we would prioritize things in our new life together. We made the decision to always prioritize our marriage, second only to God. As a result, our marriage takes top priority over everything.

So here we are, two type-A personalities—previously very independent individuals—who have come together. Now, based on how we've chosen to prioritize, we always have to consider the other person before scheduling anything. Imagine that. Isn't that what marriage entails, though? Of course it does, or at least it should. But as newlyweds, as odd as it sounds, it was quite difficult at first. For one thing, I was simply used to just doing what I had to do when I had to do it, no questions asked. Joseph, on the other hand, was used to people contacting either him or his assistant to inquire about his availability to preach, to speak, or to do x, y, or z; and if he was free, he could do it! Period. Seems fairly straightforward and harmless, right? Well, yes. That is, until I tell you that very early on in our marriage I frequently found myself frustrated because I had no idea what my husband's schedule was and often that very schedule, which I was unaware of, actually included *me* participating in or attending the event as well. This situation didn't always make for polite discussions. So you can see how things could get really convoluted, especially since I too have my own calendar with a separate schedule and list of events I have agreed to attend. We realized very quickly that if we failed to figure out a system for scheduling our respective lives, we would end up adding to the existing chaos, causing further frustration for us as a couple.

### *My Schedule, His Schedule, Our Schedule*

In a way, we were forced to sit down and figure out what OUR system would look like. We had to ignore what everyone else expected or wanted us to do, or what was easier for the staff. We knew we needed to do what was right for us. It was then that we decided that we would always prioritize our marriage and schedule everything else around that. Our marriage was and is this sacred entity that we protect like a mother bear protects her cub. It may sound somewhat over the top to some, but when other people are constantly placing demands on you, you really have to learn to be firm and protective of your time—always being polite, yet still firm and protective.

Joseph and I have managed to develop a "family" scheduling system. We wait to confirm big important appointments until after we've spoken to each other and checked our respective calendars, which by the way we both have access to on ALL of our electronic devices. One of the major issues we identified early on is that often our schedule is much more complex and fluid than it looks on paper—AND it's constantly changing. As a result, it's much easier and poses less risk of over-scheduling if we communicate with each other directly. In this day of technology we either call, e-mail, or text each other—whatever works fastest for that moment. It's important to note that doing so is not about either of us allowing the other person to dictate what we do in our life or with our time; rather, it is about recognizing that the "two" have now become "one" and can no longer operate like one person's personal schedule is all that matters. There's someone else to consider here.

The "two" have become "one" and can no longer operate like one person's personal schedule is all that matters.

For example, early on when we failed to communicate, I might try to schedule an event on a night that Joseph had something special planned for us or on a day he had an event scheduled that he was really hoping I would attend or vice versa. I see checking with Joseph to confirm before scheduling more as a simple courtesy—to my spouse and to my marriage. This process has made a significant difference in our ability to balance our schedule around personal time we put aside for "just us" to spend together, as well as those important events we wish to share with each other.

Joseph does a great deal of traveling for preaching engagements all over the country. I am fortunate enough to work in a department within the hospital where we schedule the physician coverage in advance for the entire year. Because our hospital operates on an academic calendar, the scheduling for the department usually occurs in the early spring. When that time of the year comes, Joseph and I always sit down with our schedules and we go through the year month by month, and I make every attempt to schedule my work weeks around his travel schedule so that we can be in the same place as much as possible. When he's in Nashville, I try to schedule time to work. This may seem counterintuitive, but we do this so that when he's scheduled to be out of town, I can plan time off so I can travel with him. Obviously, this doesn't always work, but we make every effort to do it. If we didn't, we could literally spend well over half of the year apart, with him traveling and me working in the hospital. On those days when I do have to work while he is traveling I simply schedule those as my hospital call nights, where I spend the night in the hospital. With the two systems I just described to you, Joseph and I are able to travel together at least 80-85 percent of the time. Even with this, we are both still able to do everything else our regular work schedules demand of us.

Granted, your spouse may not travel as much as Joseph or at all for that matter. The takeaway here is just that at the end of the day if you don't take the time to sit down and figure out a plan or formula that works for you and your family, you may find yourself busy, all right—but not necessarily busy doing those things that actually matter to you. You will be left wondering where all the time went. You have to figure out a way to dictate your schedule and prioritize the people and things that are important to you, as opposed to allowing your schedule to dictate you.

### *When It Quits Working, Reevaluate*

We've also learned that during those times when things get overwhelming, when chaos starts to rear its ugly head, and when balancing begins to feel more like stumbling and fumbling, it's time to reevaluate the various things we each have on our plate. Joseph and I made a promise to each other that if the pace of our life ever becomes overwhelming and begins to disturb our marriage, we will have to look at what's on our respective plates and let something (or some things) go. Indeed, it seems a bit daunting to contemplate having to cut back on anything that you are doing, especially if you are doing what you enjoy, but for us NOTHING is more important than God, our marriage, and our families.

### *That "One More Thing"*

People around you don't necessarily know what your schedule looks like when they are asking you to do "just one more thing." All they know is what you tell them, and that is either yes, you can or no, you cannot. One thing I came to realize is that people will continue to ask you to do things and give you more and more responsibility as long as you say yes. These are the little foxes that add to the chaos. One of my mentors in Boston had to teach me that it's really okay to say no or no, thank you. And actually, for the benefit of your sanity and survival, it's imperative that you learn to do just that. You cannot do everything and do it well. So being able to discern what you've been called by God to do or participate in versus what other people are calling you to do is imperative. We know that whatever God asks you to do He will make provisions for. He will also give you the grace, strength, and stamina to complete the task in the spirit of excellence. If you allow Him to, He will guide you in and through every task. As my husband always says, "God will allow you to have a burning for it, without allowing that thing to burn you out."

Managing the chaos definitely takes a great deal of effort and planning. It certainly does not happen by accident. Together, we are busier today than we have ever been before. However, because we are both planners, we've managed to create a system that works in the context of our careers and for our respective personalities. But most important (to show you how God works), because we have aligned our priorities with His and kept Him and our marriage central to everything we do, things seem to have become more manageable—even easier at times. Our plates are certainly full. We don't see things letting up anytime soon, but Joseph and I both know that as long as we continue to prioritize our marriage and keep God central, He will make a way for us to not only function but flourish in the midst of the chaos.

****

## ORDERING CHAOS CAN BUILD RESOLVE

LET'S BE CLEAR. CHAOS IS A PART OF LIFE. Many people ask God to remove it completely, but I believe that God allows it to build character in us. Chaos strengthens our prayer life and our resolve. But peace is not the absence of tension. Peace is the presence of revelation in the midst of chaos. The disciples ultimately experienced peace in the storm because Jesus was on board. This is the revelation that we need today. Keep Jesus on your ship. Whether it's a relationship or a friendship, having His presence is critical to surviving chaos. A lot of couples attempt to make it without Him, but He is the only one who can bring peace to the chaos.

As you consider the ramifications of this revelation, remember to build yourself up in the Word of God. As you develop schedules that synchronize and systems that are flexible, make sure you make Jesus the central figure in your relationship. In our marriage, there have been times when we have been completely overwhelmed by the demands of the day. It's in those moments that we held on to the knowledge that we had Someone who could speak to the chaos when our faith was too weak to do so.

God desires peace in our lives. When there is peace in our lives, there is peace in our homes. When there is peace in our homes, there is peace in our communities. You have the ability to order the chaos and be the couple of destiny God is calling you to be. Don't allow yourselves to be victims of the chaos; rather, get victory within the chaos. You and your mate were born to bring order. Regardless of the challenges you may experience, remember that you have been empowered to be productive and witness in the midst of it.

## Talking Points

1. How comfortable are you with chaos and disorder in your life generally? Are you the kind of person who likes your home or office desk to be organized? How much clutter is OK with you? with your spouse?

2. Share together how organized your home was growing up. Was your room usually clean and neat? Or was it a disaster waiting to happen?

3. Type-A personalities are people who are driven to succeed and be number one, who won't quit until they get what they want, who want or need

to be in charge, who are generally intense, and who think they have the wherewithal to make it happen. Type-B personalities are people who are usually more laid-back and relaxed, who let things just happen or just roll off their back. There are other differences, but both types of people can be leaders; both can be successes or failures; and both can lead happy, fulfilled lives. Of the two types, which more closely defines you and your spouse? How does knowing your mate's cadence both help and complicate your marriage?

4. Peace is not the absence of conflict but the presence of revelation in the midst of conflict. The presence or absence of peace influences how we handle conflicts. What conflicts are going on in your lives now? with each other? family? friends? work? church? community? Which are most important, and how are you addressing them?

5. How successful are you at inviting Jesus into your boat? Are you listening and thinking about what Jesus would do in your situation?

6. Reread the story of Jesus in the boat in Mark 4. What would it have been like to be a disciple with Jesus in the boat? What would it have been like to be watching the scene unfold from the shore? What do you suppose Jesus thought about his disciples afterward?

7. What is a storm to one person may not be a storm to another. Promise that you will listen to what your spouse considers a storm and help him or her keep focused on letting you and Jesus help.

## Chapter 10

# Great Expectations

Every relationship of destiny has great expectations. As a couple, we can expect to do greater things than we've done before. Once you've been intentional about growing in strategic areas, your level of expectation increases. One of the saddest things we witness is couples who don't see a future beyond their challenges. Many couples come together and forget that challenges will come. They expect failure, so they are tempted to change relationships like they change magazine subscriptions. When you are in pursuit of a relationship of destiny, you expect to see it through. The poem "See It Through" by Edgar Guest says it so well.

> When you're up against a trouble, meet it squarely, face to face;...
> You may fail, but you may conquer; see it through!

This poem reminds us to persevere through the challenges of life, knowing that life gets better up the road. We are keenly aware that God has us on a trajectory that will exceed our expectations. With this knowledge we are doing everything possible to prepare ourselves for what's ahead.

When you live in expectation, you don't focus on the past. You move beyond the baggage and issues that have limited your potential and embrace the future with optimism. You must guard your relationship against a spirit of pessimism, which can rob you of God's best for your life. See yourself in a preparation stage and know that God is allowing you to experience things to strengthen you and give you the wisdom necessary to function where He is taking you, because what you are going to is far greater than what you are going through. Remember, the devil can never kill what God wants to do, but the devil can make it so difficult that you will surrender it yourself.

## Joseph's Story

One of the many blessings Stephaine and I enjoy is that we believe God wants the best to happen in our lives. We truly embrace what God desires to do in our lives. We embrace every crisis as well as every blessing. We know that God has a plan in everything He allows. I tell people, "If God allows it, blessings are in it." *When you have great expectations in your relationship, you don't wallow in your RIGHT NOW; you live in your NOT YET.* The reason a lot of people in your past didn't appreciate you and took you for granted is that they only saw your *right now*. If people are not spiritual, they are unable to see you beyond the challenges and conflict. They are unable to see you transcending certain situations and being productive. It is important to remember that they are not your destiny. I will say it again: *God brings relationships of destiny together for your NOT YET, not your RIGHT NOW.*

### *Live into Your Not Yet*

As Stephaine and I grow together, we are constantly reminded of why God brought us together. Our ability to support each other now and embrace where we are both going is what sustains us through the challenges. You cannot get bogged down with the trivial matters and forget the larger picture. God is going to do some amazing things in your life. He was strategic in bringing you together with this amazing person. We are all like clay in the hands of the Potter. We are being molded. We are being fashioned and shaped according to His will. Every day, He is taking things out of us and adding things to us to manifest His will in our lives. As we submit our lives to His will, our relationships will be in submission. This is what Paul means in Ephesians 5:21 where he says, "[Submit] yourselves one to another in the fear of God."

Stephaine and I recognize the tremendous responsibility we have to be good stewards of the opportunities that God affords us. We must help others as we achieve our goals. We must give back as we move forward. We must walk in integrity and realize that the higher God takes us, the more we become a target of the enemy. Remember Luke 12:48, "Unto whomsoever much is given, of him shall be much required." We've learned to embrace the complexity of our lives. We came to the conclusion that our blessing rests in the reality that our lives are not our own. We belong to God, individually and as a couple. What He desires to accomplish through us motivates us and keeps us fighting for our marriage. If you don't have great expectations for your relationship, you will never fight for it.

### *Live to Change the World*

As you have read this book and have, hopefully, been moved by our story, please recognize that your story can inspire others. Stephaine and I are just vessels God uses to show others His love in the earth. Relationships of destiny are designed to exceed expectations. These relationships are designed to break curses and overturn negative statistics. Imagine that. There is something God has deposited in you and someone else that's designed to change the world. We all play a role in effecting change. You have a powerful testimony. Allow others to know your story. Share it as we have shared ours. People need to know that we struggle like they struggle. They need to know that we have contemplated giving up as they have. They need to see our faith in the midst of it all, transcending negative forces and rising to places of optimism and perseverance.

When we set out to write this book, Stephaine and I realized that in order for it to be effective, we had to be transparent. So many Christians shy away from transparency because we fear what people will think of us. There is power in our story, and we want folks to know that couples of destiny have to work every day on their relationships. The devil is no respecter of persons. He attacks us as he attacks you. We just continue to choose to work together through strategic planning to overcome him and achieve our objectives.

### *Create a Vision of Destiny*

One of the most important things you and your mate can do is establish a vision. A vision statement serves as a guide to your marriage about where you are going as a couple. Where do you see yourselves in two years or ten years? This vision keeps you on track and motivates you when life gets tough. It gives you talking points when planning or making your next big decision. Stephaine and I have found our vision statement very helpful. The vision will come to pass if you are intentional about putting things in place to guard it. Many of us have faith, but we forget that we need works as well. Faith needs a corresponding action if it is going to be effective. You can expect great things all day long, but if you don't put in the work, nothing is going to happen. Greatness doesn't happen because you think it should. Remember, life doesn't owe any of us anything. God has given all of us gifts, and those gifts must be used to His glory. We must work together as couples if our relationships are going to be those of destiny.

### *Your Destiny Represents God Too*

I've heard it said so often that marriage takes work. It does. You cannot buy into the illusion that once you get married all the issues are going to go away. You can't be naïve and believe that every day will be bliss and no challenges will be present. This is why so many marriages end in divorce. Couples set themselves up for failure; some even go into marriage expecting it. To align your expectations with God's, you must be a spiritual couple equipped with God's Word. You must be a praying couple. You cannot allow your relationship to become complacent. You have to keep striving for excellence. Stephaine and I make a habit to strive for excellence in all we do. We don't just represent ourselves. We represent God in all we do.

Ephesians 3:20 says, "Now unto him that is able to do exceeding abundantly above all that we ask or think." We all desire that God will do great things in our relationships. We have our list of things we want to accomplish, and we work hard toward that end. What Stephaine and I have come to understand is that God is in the business of blowing your mind. Just when you think you are reaching toward one level, God will take you to an entirely different one. We've learned to be open to whatever God wants to do. We realize that every level requires another level of preparation. We can always sense when God is about to elevate us because the attacks get greater. Like a great team, we buckle down, run our game plan, and come out victorious every time. We expect to win because we are champions. Whether or not you realize it, you are champions. You have overcome so much to be where you are. God brought both of your stories together so you could be a witness to others.

****

## Stephaine's Story

Anyone can get married—putting on a wedding dress or suit and walking down the aisle in front of your family and friends, declaring your undying love, exchanging rings followed by vows and a big kiss—guess what, anyone can do that. That's not what makes a marriage. People get married every day, but not everyone is prepared for or even desires marriage. Why? Because marriage takes WORK. Some people take steps toward marriage under the false pretense that being married is about perfectly rosy days and happily ever after, but it's not. Marriage is a choice. Every day is a choice. Either you choose to work as a team with your mate to strive for the type of marriage that God has ordained for you, or you choose not to. Either way, the choice is up to you. Marriage is amazing. It's a wonderful experience that I would recommend to everyone who is blessed with finding the right person, but anyone who tells you that marriage is easy and always perfect and filled with laughter is pulling your leg.

### *Marriage Is a Process*

Marriage is also a process; it's not an event. It's an ever-evolving, changing entity. Over the last two years, we have seen each other mature to a whole other level within our marriage. Things that used to bother us now make us laugh, mainly because we know where each other's heart is. We know at the end of the day that we both love each other tremendously and neither of us is perfect. We make mistakes. We say silly things that we don't mean the way they sound when the words come out. But when you know that a person loves you and would never intentionally hurt you, you learn that it's okay to not sweat the small stuff. EVERYTHING is NOT important. It can't be. Important things are important and the rest—well, it can wait.

The day we realized what we had in each other, we both told each other that we were not going anywhere. When we got married, we made a covenant with each other and with God to be in our marriage "until death do us part," and we will do just that. Whatever happens in our marriage, we are here to stay. If we argue or get upset at each other, it would behoove us to sit, talk, and come to some solution that makes sense to the both of us. Otherwise we would just be two really angry people walking around the same house. The longer it takes to talk and remedy an issue, the longer it takes to heal and move on. What's the point of that? Sometimes we do force ourselves to sit and talk because we understand the benefits of open, honest communication.

Truthfully, in the beginning, marriage was fairly difficult. Not the loving part but the transition, the coming together as one, the merging our lives and always thinking of someone else in the midst of the chaos. Things were quite challenging at times. I kept thinking, OK, if I can just keep this up until things slow down.... Then days would turn into weeks, and weeks into months, and I finally realized—this is it. This is us. This is our life! It's only with this realization that we were able to develop specific strategies and compromises to help us not lose ourselves or our marriage in the midst of everything else. Now, as we have completed two full years of marriage, we laugh a lot more. We have systems in place that work for us. We've found a cadence. We enjoy each other's company. Life is good. If I had to do everything all over again just to get back to where we are today, I would—gladly.

Whenever I think of my husband, I just start grinning from ear to ear. Joseph and I are similar in so many ways. We complement each other in so many other ways. Where I'm weak, he's strong. Where he is weak, I am strong. We lean on each other when we need to and even when we don't. We laugh—and cry—together. We are tremendously supportive of each other and our respective careers, dreams, and goals. Although he knows how to push my buttons and I know how to push his buttons, he's my number one cheerleader, and I am his.

You can see that Joseph and I certainly are not perfect people. We do not have a perfect marriage, nor do we pretend that we do. But I can certainly say that without a shadow of a doubt we ARE perfect for each other. Joseph often says we were anointed to be with each other. Think about that for a moment. When he says that, he's not necessarily talking about all of the fun, cutesy stuff of marriage. Rather, he is referring to the difficult things. The fact that things I do that would drive anyone else crazy, he embraces and loves, and vice versa. Joseph gets me and all of my quirkiness. The fact is that I ask a million and one questions about EVERYTHING to the point of annoyance because I'm just very inquisitive, but he tolerates it and answers every question. When I

We lean on each other when we need to and even when we don't. We laugh—and cry—together.

walk in the door at home from a long day's work, I drop everything in one spot—none of which belongs there. He just smiles despite the fact that he always puts things down in their assigned place. I will drive my car until the low fuel light is on, but he just gives me yet another warning that doing so is not safe and makes sure that somehow my gas tank is full the next time I get into my car. I could go on and on and on.

One thing I know for sure is that God doesn't make mistakes. When He brings two people together, there's always a method to the madness. Joseph and I know that we were brought together not just for us, but rather so we could be a blessing to others. There is no doubt that God is taking us to new heights—together. Sitting here even now I can feel God moving in our lives. He is so good. His grace and mercy abound. When God brings two people together, it means that the plans He has for one include the other. Moving forward TOGETHER is the only way to reach the destiny God has ordained for your life. What you bring to your spouse; how you pour into your spouse; how you build your spouse up on the inside, making him or her stronger, better—all of that affects your ability to get there. If God has allowed it, it's got to bless you. So hold on to your seat: your destiny as a couple awaits.

And to all the ladies who are still waiting on their mates, God has not forgotten about you. He has already chosen your spouse. It's only a matter of time. Patience is a virtue—trust me, it's worth the wait. In the meanwhile, just be you. Focus on you and your goals and what you want out of life. Sometimes when we feel like we are waiting on God, it's actually God who is waiting on us. Dare to trust Him. Dare to believe that He can do what He said He can do. You are a queen. Make sure YOU know your value. You are a child of God. He makes no mistakes. You are where you are for a reason. Pray that God might reveal the reason to you so you can move on. Your destiny awaits.

****

## YOU ARE BETTER TOGETHER

EVERY DAY WHEN YOU WAKE UP, expect something to happen in your life. Expect God to blow your mind. God has great plans for your life together. Relationships of destiny live in expectation of God's next move. As you walk in obedience and submission, you will discover what God will trust you with. God loves you so much. He wants you to be happy, at peace, and prosperous. All of these things are possible when we live lives submitted to His will. In our marriage, we've learned never to limit our expectations. We keep the top off, because God keeps ripping it off with new blessings.

Relationships are intentional journeys taken together to accomplish goals. There are a lot of things you will accomplish by yourself, but there are some things you will only accomplish together. That's why God brought us together, like Abraham and Sarah. The promise is on Abraham's life, but he needs Sarah to manifest it. As they work together, the world is blessed. We feel that's our call—to continue to work together for the fulfillment of God's will on the earth. We live every day in expectation that what God promised us will come to pass. Even when we are having a difficult day, we are reminded of His promises and we press on knowing He doesn't lie. If you haven't received everything God promised you, this can be your season. Refuse to lose. Fight for your marriage. Fight for your family. Remind the devil of your commitment and that your level of expectation is too great to give up. It may be rough right now, but what's ahead of you is better than what's been. This is what we live by. This is what motivates us every day. This is what inspires us to press on. We pray it inspires you. There are great things in your future. Go get them together. You are better together—living, loving, and creating a life that matters.

## Talking Points

1. What expectations do you have for yourself? for your spouse? Are they realistic? Are you realistic? How often do you meet your own expectations?

2. Commit to spending at least ten minutes each day just catching up with what's happened to each other that day.

3. What great gifts are you are praying for God to bless you with?

4. Promise each other that you will put in the time to learn more about your spouse—what he or she needs or wants.

5. Make a list of at least four goals that you want to see happen in the next couple of years.

6. As you look toward the future, what do you see? What preparations do you need to make? Whose guidance do you need? How can you help each other achieve your dreams and goals? Where is God in the mix?

7. Pray for perseverance, patience, and wisdom to walk in God's purpose toward destiny.

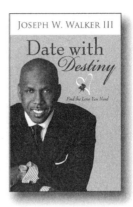

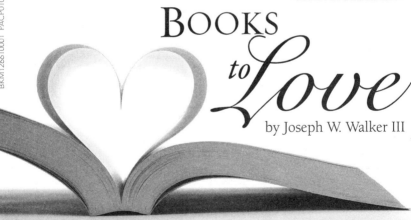